BOOKS BY
EDWIN O. REISCHAUER

Beyond Vietnam: THE UNITED STATES AND ASIA (1967)
Japan Past and Present (1947, 1952, 1964)
Wanted: An Asian Policy (1955)

THESE ARE BORZOI BOOKS, PUBLISHED IN NEW YORK BY
Alfred·A·Knopf

BEYOND

VIETNAM

BEYOND VIETNAM:

The United States and Asia

by EDWIN O. REISCHAUER

New York
ALFRED · A : KNOPF
1968

THIS IS A BORZOI BOOK
PUBLISHED BY ALFRED A. KNOPF, INC.

Published October 16, 1967

Third Printing, February, 1968

© Copyright 1967 by Edwin O. Reischauer

Library of Congress Catalog Card Number: 67-25614

Manufactured in the United States of America

Acknowledgments

This book grows out of three different kinds of personal experience: as a student of Japanese and East Asian history over the past four decades; as a resident of Asia for a total of twenty-four years; and as a government official and military officer at various times, dating back to 1941 and culminating in my experience as the American Ambassador to Japan from April 1961 until August 1966. Looking at the problems of our relationship with Asia from these three somewhat different angles of vision, I have attempted here, not to amass facts, but to seek a sense of proportion and balance in our approach to these problems.

This is not my first attempt to write about American foreign policy toward Asia. I published a book on this subject some thirteen years ago, dedicating it to my three children, Ann, Bob, and Joan, who at the time were all teen-agers. My thought was that if we would pay serious enough attention to our Asian problems their generation might be spared such disasters in Asia as the war we had just experienced in Korea. This hope proved groundless. We failed to give much thought to Asia and its problems and are now engaged in another terrible war.

When I came to write this present book, my three children and their mates, now all in their twenties, proved to be my chief stimulators and critics. Many of the ideas were argued out with them before I put pen to paper, and they were the first to read what I had written and give suggestions and corrections. I thank them sincerely for their invaluable aid. I draw back, however, from dedicating this book to their infant children. The precedent is too frightening.

I am also indebted to many other people for help in this book. The writings of a host of well-informed and thoughtful persons have provided most of the knowledge and many of the ideas presented here. The audiences to which I have spoken during the past ten months have sharpened my thinking or broadened my views by their perceptive questions and comments. More specifically, I am indebted to several friends and colleagues for reading all or parts of this book in manuscript form and for giving me many important corrections and helpful suggestions. I should like to express particular gratitude to Albert M. Craig, John K. Fairbank, Abraham M. Halpern, Henry A. Kissinger, Ernest R. May, Richard E. Neustadt, Dwight H. Perkins, Henry Rosovsky, James C. Thomson, Jr., and Alexander Woodside, and also to my wife and my eighty-eight-year-old father, Dr. A. K. Reischauer. Finally, my very special thanks to my secretary, Miss Susan Hamilton, for a great deal of typing, often under heavy time pressures, and for some very helpful digging up of facts and figures.

E.O.R.

Cambridge, Mass.
July 1967

Contents

Chapter One

The
Lesson
of
Vietnam

THIS IS not a book about Vietnam. It is about Asia and America's relationship with the more than half of mankind that lives there. Vietnam is only a small part of Asia—not quite 2 per cent in terms of population. Still, it is so much the focus of our attention these days and it so well illustrates the problems that it seems best to start there. This would be true even if the Vietnam War were to end tomorrow, because there are important lessons for us Americans to learn from our experience in Vietnam.

1. The Cost of the War

None of us needs to be reminded of the great cost to us of the war—to say nothing of the suffering it is causing the Vietnamese. We pay first in the lives of our young men and in the sorrow and suffering of their families and friends. We pay in the diversion of so much of our national wealth to destructive purposes, wealth we would rather see used for urgent constructive tasks at home and abroad. We pay dearly in national unity, because few issues during the past century have so deeply divided the American public or so troubled the American conscience. We pay a high price in our relations with other parts of the world.

This last cost is perhaps less obvious than the others

and may need some explanation. The war in Vietnam has, at the very least, slowed down the thaw in the frosty relations between us and the Soviet Union, thus affecting adversely the area of greatest peril in our foreign affairs. It has drawn down on the United States the opprobrium of many people all over the world, confirming the hostility of those who are unfriendly to us and dampening the esteem of some of our friends. Whatever the rights and wrongs of the war, there is an almost instinctive revulsion against a powerful nation, possessed of superior weapons, killing the less well-armed combatants and the defenseless civilians of a poor and backward country—and this revulsion is intensified when differences in race are involved. Television has increased the reaction. This is the first war in history that has presented its horrors in living rooms throughout the world. Because of these emotional concerns as well as rational doubts about the wisdom of American policy, the war has put a strain on our relations with our more important allies. Few of them are in full sympathy with us. Some are openly critical.

In the case of Japan, which I know best, our escalation of the war early in 1965 by our bombing of North Vietnam produced a huge popular outcry of protest. The Japanese people, who had seen their own cities wiped out by American bombers only twenty years earlier, not unnaturally identified themselves with the Vietnamese being bombed. They also felt that the United States had embarked on the same course that had earlier led Japan to ruin. Just as Japan had become entrapped in an ever expanding war against Chinese nationalism, they saw us falling deeper and deeper into the quagmire of a war against Asian nationalists on their own soil. They were certain that we would in time be drawn into fighting Communist China too and that such an expanded war would then embroil Japan because of the American bases there.

The Japanese government throughout has expressed "understanding" of the American position, but for a while in 1965 these popular reactions of fear and distaste put an almost unbearable strain on Japanese-American relations. When the United States subsequently showed its capacity to use its military power with restraint, and war did not break out between us and China, the Japanese public relaxed somewhat. Any major expansion of the war, however, would bring back the old tensions and might even wreck our warm and mutually beneficial relationship with Japan. This, of course, would be a major catastrophe, because Japan is one of the leading industrial nations of the world, and our relations with it are in the long run much more important to us than are our relations, not just with Vietnam, but with all the countries of Southeast Asia put together.

Europe is much farther away from Vietnam, geographically and emotionally, than is Japan, but the feelings there are almost as intense. Condemnation of our Vietnam policy is loudly voiced in the United Kingdom and in all our other allied countries. There are growing signs of distrust of us and a desire to draw somewhat apart. Our near neighbors in Canada react in much the same way. Any impairment of our relations with any of our major allies—Canada, Japan, and the countries of Europe—is a stiff additional price to pay for the Vietnam War. Most of us are hardly aware of this cost, but multiply it around the world, and it may compare in magnitude to the other major categories of the costs of the war to us—that is, American lives, our wealth, and our national unity.

I would not argue that we cannot go on bearing all these costs. One could callously point out that far fewer Americans are being killed in Vietnam than on the highways of our nation. Our huge and expanding economy clearly can absorb the rapidly burgeoning billions of war expenditures —though not without loss to other needy fields of activity.

The war is hardly in evidence in our city streets. Whatever it has done to our minds and hearts, it has not really affected the way we live, as did the two World Wars.

On the other hand, I do wonder how long we can stand the disunity and spiritual confusion the war has brought us and the serious threat it has posed to our worldwide interests. Nor can one say what the total bill may add up to. How many more years will we have to go on paying these high prices, and how much higher will they go if the war escalates significantly?

2. *A Negotiated Settlement*

Yes, the costs of the Vietnam War are indeed high, and our attention is naturally focused on ways to bring it to a speedy and, we would hope, satisfactory end. On this point, however, I find the prospects extremely gloomy. Chances for both a speedy and a satisfactory end to the war seem, as of the present writing, distressingly small.

Many people have placed their hopes on a negotiated settlement. Obviously we should follow every lead that shows even the faintest possibility of taking us in that direction, and we should do whatever we can to increase the chances for negotiations. Both the Administration and its critics, I feel sure, are of one mind here, though they do not always agree on what actual steps to take.

The bombing of North Vietnam is a case in point. Some have argued that the resultant increase in the pain of the war to the North Vietnamese should increase their willingness to negotiate. I find this unconvincing. In fact, the bombing may so build up their hatred and distrust of us that it increases instead their determination to go on fighting. This might be true in any country, and it is all the more likely to be true in Vietnam because of deep resentments and fear of the Occident, developed during a century of colonial domination. Thus from one point of view, chances for a negotiated settlement might be slightly enhanced if we cut down or eliminated the bombing of the North.

This, however, is not necessarily the full story. To the extent that the bombing cuts down the flow of men and munitions to the South (a point on which estimates vary widely), it reduces the capacity of the other side to wage war in the South and thus might possibly increase its willingness to negotiate. If on the other hand a reduction of the bombing permitted a substantial increase in this flow, it might from this point of view reduce the chances for negotiations.

A solution to this dilemma might be some sort of a barrier across Vietnam and Laos at the 17th parallel that would largely eliminate the military flow and at the same time remove the need to bomb the North, thus helping in two ways to increase the chances for negotiations. But is this really feasible? And, if it is, how long would it take to establish such a barrier and have it take effect? At best this would bring no speedy end to the war.

Some people feel that if we were to develop a more democratic, civilian-controlled government in Saigon, a negotiated settlement would become more possible. Perhaps so, but I have my doubts. Hanoi would have no more liking for a democratic government in the South than for the present one, and in any case the hate and distrust that separate the supporters of Saigon, civilian as well as military, from their adversaries is too great to be easily bridged. But the important point is that even at best this program too would offer no speedy solution. Given the lack of experience of South Vietnam in democracy, the divisive intellectual and social climate, the disruptions of war, and the limitations on what we as alien outsiders can do politically in Vietnam, the development of a more democratic, civilian-controlled government would be a very slow, difficult, and chancy business.

Many people rest their hope on a negotiated settlement guaranteed by some international force. This might be possible if such a force existed, one that both sides could trust and that could be brought to Vietnam in sufficient strength to underwrite a settlement. It would take tens of thousands, probably hundreds of thousands, of well-organized and well-armed men. But I see no signs of such a force. If there were one, not only Vietnam but many other world problems would be much less pressing than they are. For the present, at least, this does not seem to be a realistic solution.

However desirable a negotiated peace may be, therefore, we cannot count on achieving one, even with the best intentions in the world. Whether or not we stop bombing the North, whatever success we have in reforming the Saigon government, and however assiduous we might be in pursuing every lead toward a negotiated settlement, the chances of ending the war in this way in the near future are not great. In fact, I wonder if any sort of settlement will ever be reached until one side or the other recognizes that it faces eventual defeat.

People usually discuss what Hanoi or Washington might be willing to concede and what pressures Peking and Moscow might bring one way or the other. The problem, however, lies fundamentally with the two original and still basic protagonists in the war: the supporters of Saigon, and the Vietcong—or the National Liberation Front, as they call themselves (Vietcong means Vietnamese Communists). Perhaps the bulk of South Vietnamese belong to neither side. These are the peasant masses who only wish to be left alone. But a large part of South Vietnam's 16 million people have divided into two strongly hostile groups—one the Vietcong, apparently united in revolutionary zeal, and the other the South Vietnamese military establishment and a congeries of quarreling religious bodies and political factions held together only by a determination not to fall under Communist rule.

These two groups of millions of Vietnamese have fought each other fiercely and brutally for years. Their distrust and fear of each other run deep. Will either side be willing to lay down its arms and trust in the good faith of the other? Will either be willing to share control with the other over the territories it now dominates? And, if not, what meaning would there be to a division of cabinet seats between them? It is hard to envisage at this stage a negotiated settlement that is not virtually a surrender by one side or the other.

3. *The Choices We Face*

Perhaps I am being too gloomy. I hope that is the case. But, at least at the time of this writing, there seems no easy or certain way to reach a negotiated settlement, and, if one proves impossible, we are left with only three choices, all of them unsatisfactory. We can seek to end the war quickly by greatly increasing our military effort—that is, through major escalation—though this course would obviously run great risks. We can end the war by withdrawing our support for South Vietnam and letting the Saigon regime be overwhelmed by the Vietcong, but this, of course, would mean that we are accepting defeat. Or we can go on fighting on somewhat the present terms, in the hope that in time we could bring about a de-escalation of the scale of the war and could eventually persuade the Vietcong and Hanoi to seek a settlement, but this course means that we would go on paying the high price of the war with no clear end in sight.

The first of these choices, I believe, would give little promise of ending the war, while exposing us to absolutely unacceptable dangers. We could greatly expand the bombing of the North, say by wiping out the cities; we could land in the North, occupying the cities and cutting the lines of communication to the South; or we could use nuclear weapons. But what would we achieve by any of these acts? They would contribute relatively little to stamping out the original guerrilla war in the South. We might be able to destroy the Hanoi government as it now exists, but this would probably only mean that we then would have two guerrilla wars on our hands—the old one in the South and a new one in the North.

Any of these steps of escalation would seriously damage our position in much of the rest of the world. They might well wreck our whole relationship with Japan—and perhaps with other important allies as well. We would also be running serious risks of tangling with the 700 million people of China in a war neither side could ever win. China's Communist leaders believe that we are compelled by our very nature as "imperialists" to wish to destroy them. When, during the Korean War, we pushed into North Korean territory contiguous to China, they came out to meet us. We should assume that they might do the same in North Vietnam. And if we were to come to blows with the Chinese, no one could guarantee that the Soviet Union would not feel impelled to join in, and we then might end up with the nuclear holocaust we are all trying to avoid. Clearly a major escalation of the war in Vietnam would be absolute folly.

I find the second alternative, though more debatable, not much more attractive. There would be many ways in which we could seek to conceal the fact of our defeat. Senator Aiken has put forth the tongue-in-cheek suggestion that we declare ourselves the victors and then de-escalate the war. Others advocate that we allow ourselves to be negotiated out, presumably with the understanding that the Saigon government would be allowed to exist free of Communist control long enough to let us get out before the roof falls in on it. This would be a settlement much like what the Geneva Agreement of 1954 was intended to be for the French. Some have suggested our withdrawal into enclaves, though this would seem to me merely a surrender of South Vietnam with the additional disadvantage for us of having military bases left in this hostile land.

However our withdrawal were papered over, it would be recognized everywhere as a defeat for us, and we would have to face the consequences. The real question is what these consequences would be. All of Vietnam would fall under Communist rule—but this in itself would be only a relatively minor drawback to us, as I hope to show later in this book. Nor would the problem, as I see it, be primarily that the United States was "losing face." If one means by "face" prestige or self-esteem, then we, as overwhelmingly the strongest and richest country in the world, have, if anything, too much face. Our size, wealth, and power are already so great that in some ways they militate against us in our relations with other countries. In many they stir up suspicions and resentments against us; in others they create a sense of apathy because of over-reliance on Uncle Sam to carry all the burdens of the world. Even in a great and friendly country like Japan, I found that our very size and power made it difficult for Japanese to feel a sense of full equality with us. If only "face" were involved, we could safely withdraw from Vietnam tomorrow.

A far more important consequence of our withdrawal would be the psychological and political impact of our defeat on Southeast Asia and the whole world—and not least on the United States itself. I do not subscribe to the simple "domino theory" that if one country falls to Communism it will, in its fall, knock down the next one to it geographically and so on down the line. In a less mechanical sense, however, there is something to the domino theory.

I have pointed out that there is extreme disapproval of our Vietnam policies in much of the world, but this is not true in several of the countries closest to Vietnam. There is, in fact, strong approval in Thailand, Laos, the Philippines, Taiwan, and South Korea, and in several other Southeast and South Asian lands there is a considerable degree of quiet support, masked either by discreet silence or by an official stance of mild condemnation. Many of these countries are themselves unstable and either fear the sort of internal subversion that has torn South Vietnam apart or are apprehensive about the intentions of their great Chinese Communist neighbor and suspicious of the loyalties of the sometimes sizable Chinese populations within their borders. They would feel much less secure if the United States, after having committed itself to the fight, were forced to admit defeat at the hands of Communist insurgents. In fact, such an outcome of the Vietnam War would send a massive psychological tremor through all these countries, further threatening their stability and perhaps sharply shifting their present international orientation.

Conversely, all those who hope for Communist takeovers in the less developed countries of the world, whether in Asia or elsewhere, would receive a shot in the arm. America's defeat in Vietnam would seem to be proof positive of the Maoist doctrine that what the Communists call wars of national liberation are irresistible. It would be far better proof than Ho Chi Minh's victory over the French in North Vietnam, or the Communist triumph in China, or the sweep of Communism in the wake of the Soviet army in North Korea and East Europe, because in none of these cases was the military power of the United States directly involved. The old concept that Communism was the wave of the future, at least in the less developed parts of the world, would be strongly revived, just at a time when the wave had seemed to have spent its force and was retreating. The possibility that Communist insurgency will develop or succeed in other Asian lands depends, as I hope to show in this book, primarily on internal conditions in each country, but a clear-cut defeat of the United States in the Vietnam War would certainly be one external factor that could have a seriously adverse influence on this situation.

Some argue that these reactions could be minimized by

strenuous American efforts to build a more tenable defense line against Communist subversion on sounder terrain in Asia. Specifically it is suggested that shifting our military strength to Thailand would largely offset a defeat in Vietnam. This might be true, but I have my doubts.

Whatever our countermeasures, the defeat in Vietnam undoubtedly would change the political climate of Asia decidedly for the worse. Moreover, the proposed counterstrategy would in essence mean the further spread of American military power into areas where the Vietnam War had just shown that our type of military power was relatively ineffective. It assumes that the less developed countries would still desire a close alliance with us after having seen that an alliance with the United States was no guarantee of security from the threats that menace them most—namely, internal subversion and guerrilla warfare. To the extent that we were successful in setting up the new defense line, we might be preparing the way for further Vietnam disasters for ourselves. To the extent that such an approach by us was rejected by Asian nations, this would probably further reduce our ability to play a helpful role in Asia, even in fields other than the military.

The net results of our withdrawal from the war in Vietnam, however skillfully we might try to conceal the withdrawal, would probably be an increase in instability in much of Asia and a decrease in the influence of the United States and in our ability to contribute to the healthy growth of Asia. These adverse consequences might be felt in much of Asia for years to come.

The effects might not be limited to Asia. They might be felt in somewhat similar terms in other less developed parts of the world and might also affect our more important relations with the advanced nations. Our withdrawal from Vietnam, after all, would not have been a defeat in the sense that France, a far smaller and weaker country, had been forced to accept defeat in 1954. As has been stated all too often, we cannot be defeated in Vietnam. We simply would have decided to go back on our commitments. We might have good grounds—political, strategic, or moral—for doing this. The commitments may have been unwise in the first place. But, nonetheless, we would be welching on commitments not just solemnly made but repeated, often in grandiose overstatement, by one Administration after another. One wonders what effect this might have in other countries, such as Japan and our European allies, that have been relying on commitments made by us. It would certainly increase doubts in some of these countries about the reliability of the American nuclear umbrella, and thus it would encourage nuclear proliferation. The Japanese would praise our realism and good sense in withdrawing from Vietnam but in the next breath would point out that Americans were less likely to live up to commitments to Asian countries than to nations of the same race. Loss of face may not be a reason for not withdrawing from Vietnam, but loss of faith certainly is.

What worries me most, however, is the effect that our withdrawal from Vietnam might have on ourselves. Some Americans would justify withdrawal on moral grounds and, with renewed confidence in their own country, would return to the task of making American strength a more constructive influence for the healthy advance of the less developed countries. The more strategically minded would justify it as a sound cutting of losses in an unimportant area so that American power could be more effectively used in more important places. They would point out, not without considerable cogency, that the less developed world is of only minor immediate concern to our security and well-being and that we should cut our commitments to it and concentrate more on the advanced nations, both allied and Communist. They would argue for what might be called a sophisticated neo-isolationism of the West from the East. Already we can detect the leitmotifs of this theme in some of the leading newspaper columns of this country—the argument that after all "East is East and West is West." Asians, having their own distinctive cultures and special problems, should go their own way, presumably in poverty and turmoil, while we of the advanced nations go our own prosperous and peaceful way. One detects a longing for the simpler days when "the world" was indeed only the Occident and "the lesser breeds without the law" could be largely ignored.

These sophisticated justifications, however, would probably not be those of the bulk of grass-root Americans. They, I believe, would put a decidedly less desirable coloration on this neo-isolationism. They would justify what would otherwise seem a humiliating defeat on the grounds that all the benighted Vietnamese (I refrain from writing the actual adjectives and nouns that would be used) aren't worth the life of "one good clean Christian American boy" and that these "little yellow people" and all their ilk deserve to be left to "stew in their own juices." This attitude could all too easily turn into the worst sort of racist isolationism, which might drastically reduce our usefulness to the less developed parts of the world and might also damage our relations with the advanced nations.

One can understand the desire to conserve American strength for more constructive tasks than this unhappy war. We are all eager to save American lives and stop the carnage in Vietnam. But it is possible that in our eagerness to do this we might help produce such instability in Asia and such impotence in ourselves that the development of a more stable, prosperous, and peaceful Asia might be delayed by decades.

All these dire consequences of withdrawal are only speculation, I admit. They may be very exaggerated. No one can be sure. On the other hand, the cost of the Vietnam War is still an unfinished, if not entirely blank, check. The numbers are still being added and may in time mount up to a figure greater than the assumed cost of withdrawal. We are forced to try to judge between two largely speculative price lists.

4. *The Achievements of the War*

My own guess, as of the present, is that the less costly course will prove to be to continue somewhat along the present lines, working toward reducing the scale of the war and ending it as soon as possible, but not resorting to either extreme—withdrawal or major escalation. This is what I understand to be in general the Administration's policy, and it is for this reason that I have been basically in support of it. While I, like everyone else, keep praying that a negotiated settlement will end the war quickly on some satisfactory basis, I believe the chief hope we have for a tolerable outcome is to force the other side gradually to reduce the scale of fighting and eventually to accept some sort of reasonable settlement.

Is this slow simmering down of the war, however, a real possibility? I believe it is. We are putting tremendous military pressure on the Vietcong and have so built up our forces in South Vietnam that we cannot really be defeated in a war that remains localized there. There are signs that we may be starting to make slow progress toward getting the rural population and its produce out of the hands of the Vietcong. We are beginning to help build a broader base of support for the Saigon government. The combined military, economic, and political squeeze on the Vietcong may make it progressively harder for them to maintain the war. They are already being forced in desperation to acts that undercut their popular support. This approach to ending the war is admittedly a slow and somewhat dubious one, but it seems more promising and less hazardous than the other two.

If the gradual process of damping down the war is our best way to end it, or at least cut its costs, then our strategy should be directed primarily toward this objective. This is why we should seriously consider measures such as creating a defense barrier all the way along the 17th parallel. This is why we should direct not just verbal emphasis but our chief efforts toward political, social, and economic development in the parts of South Vietnam under Saigon's control. This is why it is important to carry out a slow but sound pacification of as much of the agricultural area of South Vietnam as possible. If the Vietcong could be denied access to the peasants and the rice they produce, their main sources of manpower and food would dry up and thus their capacity to continue the war would be sharply reduced.

Pacification, however, is a slow process, more political and economic than military. We can provide some of the military muscle, but the chief task, which is to convince people that they have more to hope for from Saigon than from the Vietcong, must be done by the Vietnamese themselves. For this the Saigon government must improve itself and its policies so as to hold out a more convincing promise of a better day to its people, and the South Vietnamese army must be retrained both politically and militarily so that it can spread the influence of Saigon more effectively throughout the country. This reform and retraining must be based not just on our alien ideas but on ideas that are appealing and meaningful to Vietnamese.

This, unfortunately, is not a quick strategy calculated to meet American election deadlines. The reasoning of our leaders in Washington, I suspect, is not very different from mine, but, being oriented toward politics in this country, they naturally pay primary attention to the influence of the war on elections here. As a consequence, they seem some-

The Lesson of Vietnam ❧ **17**

times to be grasping for quick but unsound solutions to the war. They have permitted a creeping escalation of the fighting, apparently in the unrealistic hope that some new, even if minor, pressure on Hanoi will cause a spectacular change of attitude there.

Actually, Hanoi and the Vietcong have their eyes set too on the 1968 American presidential election, hoping that it may somehow lead to an American withdrawal from Vietnam. Until this hope has been dispelled by the election itself, they are not likely to show any willingness to compromise, no matter what pressure is put on them. Thus, instead of trying to force them to give up before the election, which probably cannot be done no matter how much pressure we apply, we might better concentrate on slower but surer ways of tipping the scales against them, so that by the autumn of 1968, when they see themselves facing an American president with a four-year mandate, they may be more inclined to seek peace through negotiations. One important element of such a strategy might be the elaboration of realistic and generous terms of settlement that would give the Vietcong a tolerable alternative to an apparently endless war.

But even assuming a decided worsening of the Vietcong position by the autumn of 1968 and the formulation of realistic peace terms on our part, I doubt that a negotiated settlement even then would be much more than a cease-fire, at least at first. The Vietcong, in effect, would be suspending their attempt at an immediate military seizure of all of South Vietnam, but only in the hope that the terms of the settlement would allow them to win by other means or to recoup their strength for another try at a forceful takeover sometime in the future. Even this, however, would give South Vietnam and the world a breather—a chance to move beyond the present stalemate to a new phase in which the old war might no longer seem necessary or relevant.

I put forward these personal views of the problems we

face in trying to end the war in Vietnam with some diffidence, because I am not an expert either on Vietnam or on military matters. My purpose has been merely to bring home the fact that we are paying dearly for the Vietnam War and face a miserable selection of choices of ways to end it. The question is, to what purpose all this suffering and travail? What possibly could emerge from this war to make it all worthwhile?

Wars sometimes seem justified by their end results, but this justification hardly applies to the Vietnam War. Even the most extravagantly optimistic outcome would still leave far greater losses than gains. South Vietnam, only a tiny corner of Asia, would have a precarious chance to start restoring slowly and painfully the great damage, both spiritual and physical, done during the many years of fighting. There would be an opportunity to try to build a free society and democratic institutions, but certainly no guarantee of success. Nor would there be any guarantee that, ten or twenty years after the war had ended, political rule over South Vietnam would not be more or less what it would have been if we had never got involved there.

It is also doubtful that even a favorable outcome to the war would do much to deter Communist subversion in other less developed countries. Instead of being discouraged by our ultimate victory in Vietnam, would-be revolutionaries might be encouraged by the obvious pain of the war to the United States and the clear reluctance of the American people to get involved in further wars of this type. Whatever international goodwill might be engendered by a settlement would only slightly offset the hatred and distrust that the war had bred. Restored confidence in American power would only partially balance the harm done to our image abroad and our unity at home.

Of course, wars are usually justified more in terms of the might-have-beens they prevented than by anything positive that they produced. Some prices just have to be paid—

as in the Second World War. But is there even this justification in Vietnam? Perhaps there is, once the stakes became on one side the reliability of American commitments and on the other the Communist faith in "wars of national liberation." But the real question is whether we should have allowed the stakes to rise to that point—because it was largely our own deliberate or unwitting actions that produced this most significant of all escalations. I feel strongly that the answer is in the negative.

I have no doubt that if those who determined American policy toward Vietnam had foreseen even dimly the costs and futilities of the war, they would have made different choices at several times in the past and thus avoided the present situation, with only trifling costs, if any, to American interests. In fact, if they had made these other choices early enough in the story, our national interests in Vietnam, in Southeast Asia, and in the world would probably be less threatened than they are today.

5. *The Historical Background*

During the Second World War, President Roosevelt apparently had in mind the concept of self-determination for the colonial lands of Asia, but this admirable and realistic goal was forgotten in this country after his death and during the confused aftermath of the war. In 1945–6 I was temporarily in the State Department, and I remember very clearly that those of us with a strong interest in Asia felt that the United States should not support the restoration of colonial regimes where these had been swept away by Japanese conquest, as in Indochina, Indonesia, Burma, and the Philippines. We felt this way because of the traditional American belief in self-determination. The United States itself had been the first country in the world to escape from colonialism through a nationalistic movement for self-determination, and until the Second World War we Americans had always been the loudest critics of colonialism. It was also obvious that the tides of nationalism were beginning to run strong throughout Asia.

In the early postwar years, however, the State Department, as well as the whole government and the American people, remained overwhelmingly oriented toward Europe rather than Asia. Primarily because of our disinterest in Asia and our concern over the sensitivities and political problems of the colonial powers in Europe, we chose to ignore Asian nationalism, except in our own domain of the Philippines. Some people believed that if we were to oppose the restoration of the European empires in East Asia, this would raise suspicions that we coveted these lands ourselves and might push European nationalists into cooperation with the Communists against us in Europe. There thus were reasons in Europe for our failure to champion Asian nationalism, but in Asia this policy had dire consequences. In the long run, it was not helpful to either France or the Netherlands, permitting the Dutch to involve themselves in a messy colonial war and the French to get enmeshed in a long, exhausting, and ultimately disastrous one. At the same time, in our own relations with Asia, we started down the road that eventually brought us to our present unhappy position in Vietnam.

Ho Chi Minh, the now venerable Communist leader of North Vietnam, had already before the Second World War built up the most effective nationalist opposition to French rule in Indochina. During the later years of the war, when the French colonial regime served as the handmaiden of Japanese imperialism, Ho's Vietminh movement, with the support of substantial non-Communist elements, won a real foothold in North Vietnam. Ho operated under the protective wing of Chiang Kai-shek's Nationalist government in China and even received support from the United States. When the Japanese finally brushed aside the French in

March 1945 and then themselves collapsed in August, the Vietminh seized most of Vietnam. Chiang's forces, which took the Japanese surrender in the North, recognized the Vietminh as the *de facto* Vietnamese government in their area, and Bao Dai, the former French-controlled "Emperor" of part of Vietnam, whom the Japanese had set up as their puppet, abdicated in their favor.

In contrast, the British, who accepted the Japanese surrender in South Vietnam, used French and Japanese forces as well as their own to frustrate Vietminh control over their area before handing it over to the returning French authorities. The Chinese withdrew from the North the next February, and in March, Ho and the French worked out a compromise, whereby the French recognized Ho's regime as "a free state . . . forming part of the Indochinese Federation and the French Union," in return for permission for a limited entry of French troops into the North for a period of five years. This fragile settlement was soon shattered, and the war started with a ruthless French naval bombardment of the North Vietnam port of Haiphong in November 1946.

The fighting was to continue for about eight years. Not all Vietnamese nationalists sided with Ho and his Communist-dominated Vietminh. Many, especially religious groups such as the Catholics, the Hoa Hao, and the Cao Dai, distrusted them. The French also tried to reduce the colonial onus of their cause by dragging out Bao Dai once again and making him the head of an "independent" Vietnam "within the French Union." In 1949 the United States, alarmed by the impending Communist triumph in China and the apparently rising tide of Communism throughout the world, started to give the French substantial support, and by 1954 we were paying for 80 per cent of the French war costs.

The French, however, even with massive American aid

and the support of large elements within Vietnam, proved no match for the Vietminh, who had much less support from abroad but had Vietnamese nationalism largely on their side. Piece by piece the French lost territory and population to the Vietminh, and their war costs mounted. Eventually, after a catastrophic defeat at Dienbienphu in the spring of 1954, they realized they could go on no longer. The result was the Geneva Conference and the agreements it produced that July.

These involved, first of all, a detailed armistice agreement between the French and the Vietminh, setting up a "provisional demarcation line" at the 17th parallel, behind which each side would withdraw and across which civilians would be free to move. The agreement also set up an International Control Commission, consisting of Canada, India, and Poland, to supervise the execution of the armistice. There was also a Final Declaration orally assented to by the United Kingdom, the Soviet Union, Communist China, Cambodia, and Laos, as well as by France and the Vietminh. This document, emphasizing the temporary nature of the division of Vietnam, provided for general elections in July 1956, under the supervision of the International Control Commission, to reunify the country.

There are many differing interpretations of the true meaning of the Geneva agreements, and an abrupt shift in government in France in the middle of the conference further confused the issue. It is hard, however, to see the agreements as anything more than a face-saving formula for the French. It seems likely that all of the participants expected the 1956 elections to reunify all of Vietnam under the Vietminh. Since in 1954 the Vietminh already had most of the country in their hands, they probably would have settled for nothing less. But by 1956 the French would be well gone from Vietnam, and therefore the final collapse at that time of the side they had fought so long to maintain would no longer be a crushing blow to their pride. Defeat in two half-size pills, with a decent interval between them, must have seemed less bitter than in one big pill.

There were, at the same time, some troublesome ambiguities in the agreements. What was the point to the free movement of population to the two regroupment zones if these zones themselves were to be only transitory? Certainly the 900,000 North Vietnamese, largely Catholics, who eventually fled from North Vietnam to the South must have hoped for something more than a two-year reprieve from Communist rule. There were also phrases in the agreements —"fundamental freedoms," "democratic institutions"—that have very different meanings to democratic and to Communist countries and are commonly sources of misunderstanding rather than accord between them.

The positions taken by Bao Dai's puppet government and the United States also cast shadows over the future. The former was not a party to the agreements and expressed its disapproval. The question is how much of a political entity it was in July 1954. It did not proclaim its full independence of France until the next January, and at Geneva, France accepted responsibility for ensuring that any successor to it in Vietnam would live up to the agreements.

The United States too refused to endorse the agreements, though it gave no indication at Geneva that it would oppose the elections. Before long, however, Washington was embarked on a twofold response that clearly was headed in a different direction. In September 1954 the United States organized the so-called Southeast Asia Treaty Organization (SEATO) together with the United Kingdom, France, Australia, New Zealand, Pakistan, the Philippines, and Thailand. A supplementary protocol to the treaty stipulated that its provisions for immediate consultations in the event of any threat to the area would apply specifically to "the free territory under the jurisdiction of the State of Vietnam." The implication thus was that South Vietnam would be a continuing political entity. The United States sought to make this more likely by plunging into the task of building up South Vietnam. The apparent assumption was that, relieved from the incubus of French colonialism, a non-Communist Vietnamese regime would prove stronger in the face of the Vietminh challenge than it had before.

While the Geneva Conference was in progress, Bao Dai, then in Paris, selected Ngo Dinh Diem to be his Prime Minister. Diem, who, like Bao Dai, was from central Vietnam, was a genuine nationalist and, having been out of the country, had avoided collaboration with the French during the previous four years. As a man of character and determination—and also possibly because he was a devout Catholic—he won the confidence and support of the United States government. This helped him to eliminate his rivals for power in South Vietnam. In November 1954 he ousted the commander in chief of the army, assuming thereafter direct authority over the military. By the autumn of 1955 he had broken the power of the Cao Dai, the Hoa Hao, and other religious groups and political factions that had independent military forces. That same October he deposed Bao Dai in a referendum that he no doubt would have won even if he had not rigged it to obtain 98 per cent of the vote. Diem then proclaimed himself President and thenceforth, with the aid of his close-knit family, ruled as a virtual dictator. Meanwhile the United States, now unequivocal in its support of Diem, had launched a massive program of economic aid and had started to retrain and reorganize the South Vietnamese army.

The assumption remained, however, that the elections scheduled by the Geneva Conference for 1956 would throw the South into the hands of the Vietminh. Diem obviously was determined the elections would not take place. He refused to participate in preliminary discussions in July 1955, as called for in the Geneva agreements, and, with clear American support, he ignored the date for the elections the next summer. Thus the supposedly temporary demarcation line between North and South began to look more permanent.

Diem proved surprisingly successful in pulling the South together and building up a reasonably effective political system, but he failed to gain much popular support. His ruthless suppression of identifiable remnants of the Vietminh and all open opponents of any sort turned South Vietnam into something of a police state. His heavy reliance on Northern Catholics irritated the largely Buddhist Southerners, who had old resentments against Northern domination. He alienated the peasantry by reducing their rights of self-government, by enforcing rent payments the Vietminh had canceled, and by carrying out only a pallid land-reform program in return. He enraged the ethnic minorities, the primitive tribes of the hills collectively known as Montagnards, by settling Vietnamese on their traditional lands and attempting to assimilate them culturally.

Armed resistance broke out sporadically, led at first by militant remnants of religious communities and various political groups, including, no doubt, former Vietminh supporters. Guerrilla activity increased markedly in the second half of 1959, and the next March so-called "veterans" of the Vietminh publicly announced their determination to get rid of Diem and the Americans by force. About 120,000 Vietminh soldiers and their families had gone North after the 1954 division of the country, but still larger numbers of Vietminh supporters had remained in the South, and these, now called by Saigon the Vietcong, increasingly became the heart of the movement against Diem. Relying on guerrilla tactics and terror, especially the assassination of uncooperative local leaders, they rapidly spread their control over large parts of rural South Vietnam.

It is still not clear what Hanoi's role may have been in the early days of the anti-Diem movement. Although outraged at the flouting of the Geneva agreements, Hanoi remained curiously passive, at least on the surface. Ho had his hands full trying to get his half of the country on its feet. He faced a permanent food deficit. Communist agricultural policies as usual produced agrarian unrest, and actual uprisings had to be put down by military forces in the autumn of 1956. At about the same time the relatively free press proved to be highly critical of the government and had to be tightly muzzled. Economic recovery remained slow. Perhaps for these reasons, Hanoi at first gave no open support to the insurgency in the South. This does not mean that the North did not surreptitiously order or encourage at least some of it, but the exact combination of spontaneous peasant uprising, organized revolution by Southern Vietminh, and plotting and training of guerrillas in the North is still largely a matter of conjecture.

By 1960, however, Hanoi had become openly involved in the guerrilla war in the South. In September it gave its public blessing to the insurgency movement, and the next year it began to infiltrate into the South some of the Southern Vietminh who had moved to the North after the 1954 agreements. In 1964 Hanoi further escalated its involvement by starting to send units of the North Vietnamese army into the battle.

Diem held his own for a while against the Vietcong and against the disgruntled elements among Saigon's supporters, but by 1963 the military tide was running heavily against him, and his political support, both in South Vietnam and among Americans, was eroding rapidly. There had been an abortive military coup against Diem as early as November 1960, but in May 1963 a much more serious and prolonged Buddhist uprising broke out. When the United States finally made clear its loss of confidence in Diem, the military murdered him on November 1, setting up a junta in his place. But getting rid of Diem did not produce political stability. The 1963 coup was followed by several abortive and two successful coups within the next two years. There were also repeated popular disturbances, culminating in a large-scale Buddhist uprising in the spring of 1966. At the same time, economic and political conditions in the countryside deteriorated under the impact of the increasing scale of fighting.

The military situation throughout South Vietnam also continued to deteriorate, despite a steady increase of American military support. At the end of 1960 only 800 American military men were in Vietnam, but at the time of President Kennedy's assassination, not quite three years later, there were 15,000. When President Johnson was re-elected in the autumn of 1964, he faced a choice between the possible collapse of Saigon and massive American participation in the war. He chose the latter course, starting the bombing of the North in February 1965 and building up American military forces in Vietnam to more than 400,000 over the next two years. Only then did the military situation in the South take a turn for the better, but by then, of course, the United States was trapped in the present unhappy situation.

6. *The Historical Alternatives*

I have given this sketchy history of Vietnam since 1945 simply to allow us to look at the might-have-beens had we made some different choices. Here again we venture into pure speculation, but this is necessary if we are to draw any lessons from our Vietnam experience.

The obvious alternative—and it has been the same one all along and probably the only real alternative to what has happened—was to allow Ho and his Communist-dominated Vietminh to take over the whole of Vietnam. This would have happened early in the story if the United States had made quite clear in 1945 that it did not approve of the revival of colonialism in Asia and would give it no support. It would still have happened if we had not given massive aid to the French war effort after 1949. It would have happened if we had been willing to support the Geneva agreements and had not tried to build up a permanent regime under Diem in South Vietnam. It would have happened if we had not steadily increased our military commitments to South Vietnam between 1960 and 1963. It would have happened if we had decided against massive participation in the war in the winter of 1964-65. Thus, under each of our last four presidents, decisions were clearly made, even if not fully thought out, to reject this one obvious alternative.

What would have happened if at any of these moments of decision we had chosen the alternative? If we had clearly favored Vietnamese nationalism over French colonialism in 1945, it seems obvious that Ho in short order would have established effective control over the whole of Vietnam. He probably would have set up the same sort of dictatorial, oppressive, Communist rule over all Vietnam that he actually did over the North. He would probably have encountered much the same sorts of problems he did in the North, and the economic progress of Vietnam would have been slow, though of course not as slow as in a war-torn land.

The society and government of this unified Vietnam would probably not have been something we would have approved of, but we have not found much we could approve of in the society and government of a divided Vietnam either. Quite possibly a unified Vietnam under Ho, spared the ravages of war, would have gone at least as far toward the evolution of a stable and reasonably just society as has the divided, war-torn land we know today.

For us, however, the question is what that sort of Vietnam would have meant in international politics. I believe it would be safe to assume that it would have been a highly nationalistic Vietnam. By the same token, I believe it also would have been free of Chinese domination. The Vietnamese have instinctive fears of their great northern neighbor. While they have always admired and imitated China, for more than a millennium they have had a deep national tradition of resistance to its domination. If they had had no specific reason to fear or resent us, the chances are that their fears and resentments would have come to focus on China, whether or not it too were Communist.

It seems highly probable that Ho's Communist-dominated regime, if it had been allowed by us to take over all Vietnam at the end of the war, would have moved to a position with relation to China not unlike that of Tito's Yugoslavia toward the Soviet Union. Ho, like Tito, had had cordial wartime relations with us. He apparently expected our continued friendship and had more to hope for in economic aid from us than from China. He and his associates were ardent nationalists and probably had deeper fears and suspicions of the Chinese than the Yugoslavs had of the Russians. While such a Vietnam might have been more circumspect and respectful toward China than Tito has been toward the Soviet Union, it would probably have been even more fiercely independent. The way in which Hanoi has sought to maintain its independence of Peking and Moscow, despite the military dependence on both forced on it by the protracted war with us, suggests how strongly independent a Communist Vietnam would have been, if not pushed by these military necessities.

Would such a Communist regime in all Vietnam have been a serious menace to its neighbors or to world peace? I doubt it. A Communist takeover in all Vietnam shortly after the end of the war would probably have seemed to the rest of the world no more of a Communist triumph than the successive victories of Communists over anti-Communists that have taken place in Vietnam since 1945. It is hard to believe that a united Communist Vietnam would have had any more harmful an influence on Laos than a divided war-torn Vietnam has had. Laos and Cambodia might have fallen under Vietnamese influence, but this at least would have kept them out of Chinese control. Or, possibly, Cambodia's traditional animosity toward Vietnam would have induced it to veer farther away than it has from association with the Communist nations, if South Vietnam too had been Communist. Thailand would probably have been less adversely affected by an entirely Communist Vietnam than it has been by the prolonged war there. Meanwhile a united, strongly nationalistic Vietnam, while paying lip service to Communist China, would probably have served as a far more effective dike against the southward extension of Chinese power and influence than has a North Vietnam forced into military dependence on China and an unstable South Vietnam. And this general situation in Vietnam and Southeast Asia, which would have been so much less unsatisfactory for us than what we have today, would have been achieved without any of the terrible costs that have mounted so high.

At each succeeding stage this relatively tolerable alternative becomes a little less attractive and more problematic. Still, if we had not given the French strong support after 1949 and had thus permitted their more rapid collapse, the outcome might not have been much worse than that outlined above. Even if we had supported the Geneva agreements in 1954, the story might still at that late date have been essentially the same. This was the point where, because of a grievous misreading of Asian history, we made our greatest and most obvious blunder.

Once we had committed ourselves to Diem and had underwritten his refusal to go through with the unification of Vietnam, the choices became much more difficult. Both Hanoi's dependence on China and its animosity toward us increased. And bit by bit our commitments in Vietnam built up to the high stakes that now would make our withdrawal and acceptance of defeat so extremely costly. Even so, if we had realized how high the price of the war was going to mount, we might have chosen to relinquish the stakes rather than raising them. This might have been advisable when Diem started to founder in the face of mounting discontent and insurgency or when the successor regimes to Diem proved little more viable. Even as late as the autumn of 1964 we might have decided against massive military participation in the war if we had realized what the costs during even the next three years would prove to be.

7. *Hindsight and Foresight*

All this may be reasonably clear now, but was it foreseeable early enough to be of any help to us? We are all better at hindsight than at foresight. In this case, however, I believe we could have had a clear enough idea of the dangers of the course we were following and enough of an understanding of the alternative to have made wiser choices—if we had only bothered to study the problems we faced, carefully and in historical depth.

I say this because, as mentioned above, I was among those who were enough interested in Asia in 1945 to take its problems seriously and therefore could see that its future lay not in a revival of colonialism but in nationalism. I am even more insistent on this point because, in the traumatic aftermath of the Communist sweep through China and the painful Korean War, just at the time when the United States was making some of the most crucial decisions that were to lead to the present unhappy position in Vietnam, I and other specialists in the Asian field attempted to call attention to the lack of a well-thought-out policy toward Asia and the consequent dangers of falling into just the sort of trap that Vietnam has become.

During the spring and summer of 1954, I labored on a book that appeared early the next year under the rather dramatic title *Wanted: An Asian Policy*. My publisher, in an uncharacteristic lapse into a cliché, labeled it an "agonizing reappraisal," but I looked upon it more as a call for a first appraisal. "Instead of attempting to say the last word," as I put it, I was "more interested in saying a first word in attempting to stimulate the free debate that is necessary if we are to develop an adequate Asian policy." That was the meaning of the title. We had not yet come to grips with the basic problems of our relationship with Asia and therefore were headed for more trouble.

Perhaps a few paragraphs from what I wrote in 1954 will best show that even then the Vietnam tragedy was not entirely unpredictable. They sound dated, of course. I call Vietnam by its old-fashioned name of Indochina, and, influenced by the spirit of the cold war when it was at its coldest, I refer to Communism as if it were a single great wave threatening to sweep over Asia. Still, these passages show that the shoals we were drifting toward in Vietnam could already be clearly perceived in 1954:[1]

> Indochina is the classic case in which the Communists have utilized nationalism effectively against us. There we find a sobering example of the weakness of defending the *status quo* against the offensive of Communist-dominated nationalism. In Indochina the French empire, the largest remaining traditional colonial power, backed by the financial and military resources of the United States, was pitted in a frustrating and at best indecisive battle against the Communist Vietminh. . . .
>
> Many Indochinese have been willing to fight with fury and to die with heroism for the Vietminh cause, but few have shown a comparable enthusiasm for the French-backed Vietnam regime. Perhaps most Indochinese remain suspicious of both sides, and a majority may fear the Vietminh Communists more than Vietnam and the French. Still, enough have actively joined the Vietminh side to give it a large and strong fighting force, while, despite all the cajoling of French administrators and the support of American equipment,

[1] From *Wanted: An Asian Policy* (New York: Knopf; 1955; Copyright by Edwin O. Reischauer), pp. 251–7, 178–9. Italics have been added.

no Vietnamese military units have had sufficient spirit to bear any great part of the load of defense. In essence, the local farm boy, fighting on his own terrain and for his own soil, was pitted against the professional soldier from across the seas. The fallen Vietminh guerrilla was much more easily replaced than his alien adversary. On Indochinese soil Vietminh-dominated nationalism appears to be more than a match for French pride or American dollars. . . .

The most disturbing aspect of the Indochinese problem is that it may now be too late for any really desirable solution. . . . We have already seen that colonial armies cannot stem the Communist tide in southeast Asia. The only hope of halting it and eventually turning it back rests with the people of that area. There can be no secure defense line in Indochina until the inhabitants of South Vietnam, Cambodia, and Laos themselves are willing and able to maintain it, and this in turn seems unlikely until they have achieved real and not merely nominal independence and on the basis of this new freedom have started to develop strong and healthy societies. But is there time at this late date to erect this one and only effective dike against communism in Indochina? Time is running out, and the creation of independent and healthy nations is at best a slow undertaking.

This is the tragedy of the Indochinese situation. If this solution of the problem had been tried ten or even five years earlier, the chances for success would have been infinitely greater than they are today. If we had had the foresight and courage in the early postwar years to persuade the French to extricate themselves soon enough from their untenable position in Indochina, the great force of Indochinese nationalism might not have fallen into Communist hands and might instead have served as the basis of nationalist regimes that would have been much more effective than the French in halting communism. . . .

Indochina . . . shows how absurdly wrong we are to battle Asian nationalism instead of aiding it. From the start the offensive was lost to the Communists, and we were forced into an extremely ineffective and ultimately hopeless defense of the *status quo.* . . . *The French failure to relinquish Indochina has put a heavy burden on the United States financially and could end by costing us dearly in lives.* . . .

If in our mind's eye we shift the scene of the recent war from Korea to some other Asian countries, the immensity of the problem of defending Asia becomes all too clear. Assume for the moment that American armies were forced to fight in Indochina and to repel enemies as strong as the Communist forces in Korea. What would the problems then be? First, we should discover that the addition of almost two thousand miles to our lines of communication from both the United States and Japan had greatly increased our supply difficulties and correspondingly weakened our punch. Both terrain and climate would be less favorable for us than in Korea, and we should find that whatever our lines of defense might be, they could be anchored by sea power only on the east and would melt away into the jungles and mountains of the interior on the west, where the advantages would lie entirely with the Communist guerrillas. And, worst of all, *we should find few Indochinese willing to fight with the ardor of our Korean allies, and at our backs would be a veritable quagmire of civilian apathy or resentment.*

If the Vietnam situation were a unique example of the United States stumbling unheedingly into trouble in Asia, one might regard it simply as bad luck. But this sort of luck has come our way all too often to be just accident. During and immediately after the Second World War we were so preoccupied first with the defeat of Japan and then with its reform that, while we planned wisely for Japan's future and executed our policies with vigor, we all but ignored our allies and the peoples we had liberated from Japanese conquest. As we have seen, we turned our backs on the problems of colonial Asia. We also hid our eyes from the obvious fact that a great civil war was inevitable in China. Americans either refused to believe that the Chinese Communists could destroy Chiang's Nationalist regime or else failed to comprehend what the consequences might be. When it happened, we did not know how to deal with the situation and ended up with a policy that minimized our influence and maximized tensions and ill will.

Korea presents an even sorrier story. We promised it independence from Japan but did nothing to prepare for this, overlooking the fact that it would be no easy task for the Koreans to build a viable political system or economy. They had been ruthlessly dominated and exploited by the Japanese for two generations and had no political traditions to look back to before that except an entirely outmoded and discredited monarchy. We allowed the country to be divided between ourselves and the Soviet Union at the outset; we entered South Korea with no plans for its future and no preparations for the tasks we faced; only slowly did we come to realize that the Russians would not permit the reunification of Korea except on their own terms of Communizing the whole country; only then did we tardily move toward developing a democratic society in the South. When the Russians, having completed their simpler task of erecting a Communist satellite in the North, announced their withdrawal from Korea by the end of 1948, we hastily followed suit, breathing audible sighs of relief. Only when North Korea, with Soviet backing, invaded the South two years later did we begin to pay adequate attention to the Korean problem, but, of course, by then it was a desperate wartime situation.

There is a distressing repetitiveness in this pattern. We fail to pay adequate attention to the basic problems we face in Asia until some catastrophe occurs, and then it is too late for any happy outcome. Even in 1954 I could write,[2] "Korea and China both reveal not simply distressing failures of American foreign policy, but frightening inadequacies in

[2] *Wanted: An Asian Policy,* pp. 23–4.

our whole approach. The United States has been less directly involved in Indochina, but the story has been essentially the same: we have been unwilling to face up to the real problem until it was too late to hope for any truly satisfactory solution. . . . We have already tasted in these three countries the bitter fruits of ignorance and indifference, but Asia contains other potential Chinas, Koreas, and Indochinas, for which we are today no better prepared than we were for these earlier disasters."

I enjoyed writing this book in 1954; it gave me a sense of having done my duty in raising the danger signals. Unfortunately the other objective in writing a book—to have people read it—was not achieved. My book sank quietly into the sea of library volumes without raising a ripple. During the Korean War, the attention of Americans had been directed toward Korea and Communist China. Every move to bring the war in Korea to a tolerable end was hotly debated, but not the broader issues of our relationship with Asia. By 1955 the fighting was over, and our attention had shifted elsewhere, leaving us little the wiser for our Korean experience. People were no longer willing to devote much attention to the on-going problems of our relationship with Asia. Storm warnings might be up in Vietnam, but we were not prepared to recognize them. We continued to drift toward new catastrophes.

Now that we are again caught in a painful and frustrating situation in Asia, our attention has swung back there, but once again our focus is too narrow. We still have not come fundamentally to grips with our Asian problems. There is a flood of debate over every conceivable move, military or political, which might help bring the Vietnam War to an end, but little serious thought is being devoted to the broader problems of our relationship with Asia that underlie the Vietnam fiasco. First things come first, the argument runs, and, until the outcome in Vietnam becomes clear, it is not necessary or even possible to rethink broader Asian policies.

This, however, is tragically wrong. After the Vietnam War is over, our interest may recede again, as it did after the Korean War, and American policy may be left to drift toward new disasters. An even more pressing danger is that while the war drags on in Vietnam we may be making the first little mistakes elsewhere that may lead us into similar tragedies. This was exactly what happened during the period when our attention was focused on Korea.

Again I can best illustrate the point by quoting from the opening paragraphs of the book I wrote in 1954. Discounting the somewhat breathless tone of anxiety—characteristic of that period—what I wrote then applies only too well to the situation today:[3]

> In recent years we Americans have often been in violent disagreement over our relations with Asian countries, but there is one point on which all of us seem to be in accord: the present state of our relationship with Asia is certainly not satisfactory. . . . Something, we feel, is wrong, but when we try to define what that something is, extraordinary differences of opinion emerge. The same set of facts about Asia seems to mean one thing to some Americans and almost the opposite to others. . . . We . . . must be approaching our problems in Asia with some very different assumptions. . . .
>
> We have often failed to see past the many distressing surface phenomena to underlying causes. We have approached problems piecemeal without adequately considering their relationship to one another or to the situation in the rest of the world. It can be said that we have had many Asian policies but not an Asian policy, and this lack is undoubtedly the primary reason for the very limited success we have had in meeting our greatest crises in Asia and our even more frightening inability to foresee them.
>
> We have still to determine what are our basic interests in Asia—what are the dangers to be avoided and the hopes to be fulfilled in that part of the world. We

[3] *Wanted: An Asian Policy*, pp. 2–11.

have reached no agreement on what really is happening in Asia, how this may affect us, and what we should do about it. We all share the desire to stop communism from spreading farther in Asia and to roll it back if possible, but this is not in itself a full policy. Not only is it a dangerous over-simplification of our Asian problem, but it is inadequate even as far as it goes, for it tells us nothing about how communism spreads in Asia or how it can best be combated there.

Unless we have a more fully developed Asian policy than this, we cannot even judge with assurance the success or failure of our specific actions, until it is too late to modify them. So long as we do not know what we are dealing with or what we can reasonably hope to achieve, we are operating in the dark. Under such circumstances we need not be surprised when apparent success turns mysteriously into failure. . . .

The guideposts of our earlier policies toward Asia mark only a faint trail on the periphery of our problems of today, when man's new mastery over space and cosmic power has stripped us of our ocean defenses, and two terrible wars have destroyed much of what little order had once been achieved in the relations between nations. . . . Asia, once so remote, has become the principal field of maneuver in a divided and precariously balanced world. It is there that we have experienced in recent years most of our major disappointments and failures in foreign policy. From this fact alone we can surmise that in Asia may lie our least understood and therefore, in the long run, possibly our most dangerous problems. . . .

In Asia in the past few years cold war has turned hot more often than elsewhere in the world and threatens to continue to do so in the future. . . . From these failures and problems in Asia have also arisen the most bitter disagreements that have divided and weakened Americans in recent years. . . .

It would be an exaggeration to say that Asia will decide the fate of the world. Rephrase the proposition but slightly, however, and it is probably true: the fate

of the world will be that of Asia; for in a rapidly shrinking world it seems unlikely that there will be more than
one destiny for humankind.

8. *The Broader Problems*

What I was trying to say in that book was that Asia was
becoming vastly important to us but we had failed to give
adequate thought to the problems it presented. We in the
United States had roughly one third of the world's wealth
and therefore the world's power, while Asia had more than
half of the world's population. And in a contracting world,
the relationship between our third of the world in terms of
power and their half in terms of population was a matter
of great significance to us and to everyone else. But we
seemed only imperfectly aware of this. Our knowledge was
dangerously thin. Much of our policy was based on unsound
analogies to the very different situation in Europe. Perhaps
even more of it was determined simply by bureaucratic drift.
Unfortunately, today, almost a decade and a half later,
all this is still true. Our knowledge remains thin. Our concepts of our interests in Asia and the problems and possibilities we face there are vague and sometimes contradictory.
Our policies are still in large part the product of unsound
analogies or blind drift. Our attention may have been drawn
once more to Asia by the pain of the war in Vietnam, but we
show no more tendency than before to come to grips with
the basic problems. We concentrate on trying to alleviate
the painful symptoms resulting from past mistakes, rather
than seeking out and curing the underlying causes of our
difficulties. If the sad story of Vietnam is not to repeat itself,
we must get a clearer idea of where we want to go in our
relationship with Asia and then shift in this direction step
by step as opportunity offers.
There is an even more immediate danger if we do not

chart a safer and more successful course through the shoals of our relationships with Asia. The American people have found the Vietnam War a deeply frustrating experience. This frustration has been reinforced by the daily presentation of the war's horrors on television. This is a new factor in society that lessens popular acceptance of the use of force. I doubt that the American public will tolerate more Vietnams, or even a long continuation of the present impasse if there is no clear hope of fairer sailing beyond it. Behind the Vietnam tornado we see the massive storm clouds of the hostility of 700 million Chinese and the forbidding fog banks of poverty and famine in India and much of the rest of Asia. The prospect seems far from promising. In frustration and despair we might react irrationally.

I have already pointed out the futility and dangers of major escalation of the present war. All along, however, there have been those who sought to respond to our frustrations in Asia by simply doing more of the same, only harder. This is a natural reaction. In the simple world of gamblers, it may make sense to try to recoup losses by repeatedly doubling the bet. But this strategy does not work in international affairs. In the case of Asia, with its huge population, tremendous diversity, and great instability, it cannot work. Vietnam has shown us all too clearly the limitation of what we can achieve by sheer military force in Asia. If it is this difficult to bring peace and stability to this one small corner of Asia, it would be folly for us to try to be the policeman of all Asia.

A major escalation of the war would only bring greater frustrations for us, but, even without this, I think the greatest danger of the present situation is that—lose, win, or draw in Vietnam—the pain of the experience may induce Americans to withdraw from Asia into the sort of Occident-centered neo-isolationism I have described above. Next to a nuclear war, I find this the most frightening prospect of all, because it could have drastic consequences for the stability and prosperity of the world for generations to come. By failing to use our third of the world's wealth and power wisely and effectively in the half of the world that needs it most, we could tragically slow down the progress of the whole world toward peace. This is an all too possible end product of the Vietnam tragedy—unless we set our minds right now to the task of thinking through our long-range relationship with Asia and discovering sounder and more effective policies than we have so far devised. Only if we can chart a wise middle course between a futile attempt to force Asia to conform to our wishes and a self-defeating withdrawal from Asia in despair can we hope to pass safely between this Scylla and Charybdis.

In discussing the lesson of Vietnam, I have held out no hope for easy solutions to the suffering there. The light at the end of the tunnel seems to me still a long way off. As we try to think through the problems of our basic relationship with Asia, however, it could be that we will gain new insights into our Vietnam dilemma. It is possible that growing understanding of the broader, long-range problem may contribute to a solution of our more immediate crisis.

Chapter Two

Our
Asian
Problem

As I said at the outset, this is not a book about Vietnam. The war there is simply the most recent and most painful symptom of an underlying malady. The real problem is that we have not paid adequate attention to our relationship with Asia. We have not determined in what ways Asia is important to us, what are the basic problems we face there, and what we can do about them.

In approaching Asia, we are like the proverbial blind men examining the elephant. Some of us have a little familiarity with bits of the animal—the trunk, tail, or left hind foot—but we lack a clear concept of the whole. We have little feel for the relative proportions of the various parts and how they fit and work together. This is what I shall strive to provide in the rest of this book. I shall try to avoid being swamped by names and details. I shall not count hairs on the lower right ear, but shall attempt to describe, even if in hazy outline, the general proportions and nature of our elephant, as I see it.

1. The Size of the Problem

We might start by considering the size of Asia. Our concept of the size of countries and regions is usually determined by ordinary maps, which of course show surface dimensions. Such maps are dominated by the great Arctic wastes of Siberia, Canada and Greenland (especially in the distortion of Mercator's projection) and by the almost empty deserts of Africa, the Middle East, Central Asia, and Australia. A hundred square miles in the Sahara or Alaska show up as big as a like area in the industrialized Ruhr, New York City, or the heavily populated lower valley of the Yangtze. Two much more significant measures of the size of countries or regions are population and productive capacity. These show two very important, though differing, dimensions of the real world and are each far more meaningful than square miles.

While I was in Japan, I devised two maps of the world showing the relative sizes of the nations of the world, one by population and the other by gross national product (GNP). I did this in order to help Japanese see their own country in better world perspective, but these maps, I feel, are equally useful for Americans. They are reproduced on pp. 48–51 of this book, because they show clearly some of the true proportions of Asia that we should keep constantly in mind.

In these two maps, I minimized ocean areas, since wide expanses of ocean are now little more significant, economically or strategically, than are narrow strips and cut countries off from one another much less than do high mountain ranges or unpopulated stretches of desert or forest. The data used were for 1964 and were in part only of approximate accuracy. The basic proportions, however, are more or less correct and have changed little since 1964, except for a further concentration of the world's population in the less developed countries and the world's wealth in the industrialized nations.

These maps show quite clearly both the scale and the fundamental nature of the Asian problem. These days the term "Asia" is commonly used to mean only the South and East Asian areas from Pakistan and India around through Southeast Asia and Indonesia to China, Korea, and Japan. On the population map, even this limited Asia looms as over half the total world. The only other part of the world that expands greatly is Europe, while the other less developed areas, such as Africa, the Middle East, and Latin America, retain roughly their normal geographic proportions.

On the GNP map, on the other hand, Asia and the rest of the less developed world shrink into insignificance. Africa looks like a Sicily off the boot of Italy, Latin America is a tail to the huge United States, and Asia dwindles to a small corner of the Eurasian land mass. Among the Asian nations only Japan, instead of shrinking, has grown. In fact, the contrast between Japan and the rest of Asia is so great that it obviously must be considered in a different category. The GNP map is completely dominated by the advanced, industrialized nations—Western and Eastern Europe, the Soviet Union, Japan, the United States, Canada, Australia, and New Zealand. The United States in particular, while maintaining its normal geographic proportions on the population map, becomes a giant on the GNP map, accounting for about a third of the total.

Here we see in graphic outline the main aspects of our Asian problem. There is an appalling contrast between the concentration of the world's population in the less developed countries and the world's wealth and power in the advanced nations. The one group consists largely of tropical or subtropical countries in the South. The other consists of northern countries, with two small offshoots, Australia and New Zealand, in the southern temperate zone. If we draw a rough line between the industrialized, modernized "North" and the unindustrialized, underdeveloped "South," we find more than two thirds of the people on the poorer side of the line but almost four fifths of the wealth

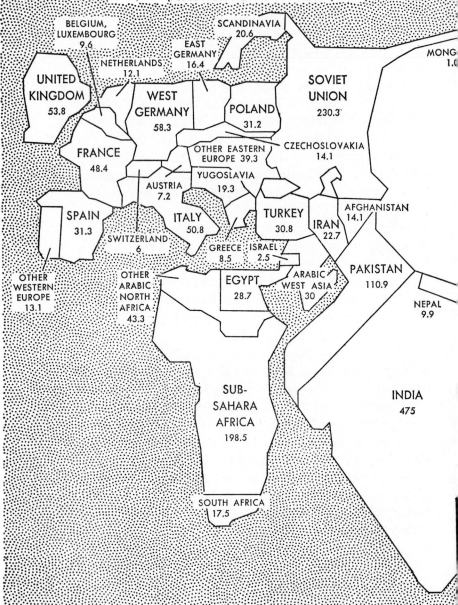

POPULATION

□ REPRESENTS 1 MILLION
(POPULATION FIGURES IN MILLIONS)

BELGIUM, LUXEMBOURG 9.6

SCANDINAVIA 20.6

EAST GERMANY 16.4

NETHERLANDS 12.1

MONG 1.0

UNITED KINGDOM 53.8

WEST GERMANY 58.3

POLAND 31.2

SOVIET UNION 230.3

FRANCE 48.4

OTHER EASTERN EUROPE 39.3

CZECHOSLOVAKIA 14.1

AUSTRIA 7.2

YUGOSLAVIA 19.3

SPAIN 31.3

ITALY 50.8

TURKEY 30.8

IRAN 22.7

AFGHANISTAN 14.1

SWITZERLAND 6

GREECE 8.5

ISRAEL 2.5

PAKISTAN 110.9

OTHER WESTERN EUROPE 13.1

OTHER ARABIC NORTH AFRICA 43.3

EGYPT 28.7

ARABIC WEST ASIA 30

NEPAL 9.9

SUB-SAHARA AFRICA 198.5

INDIA 475

SOUTH AFRICA 17.5

CEY 16

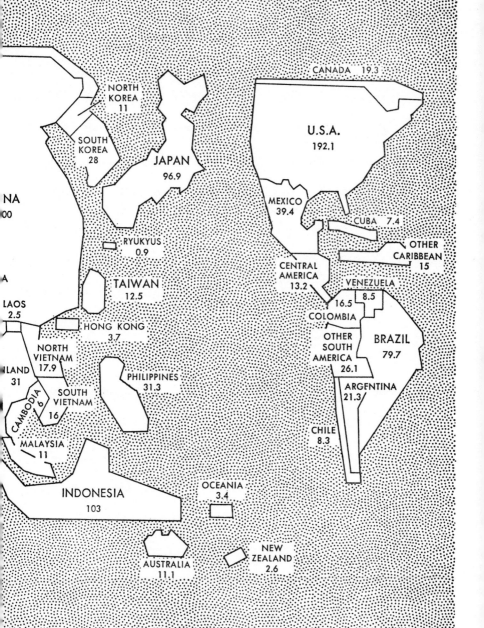

NORTH KOREA 11

SOUTH KOREA 28

JAPAN 96.9

NA 00

A

LAOS 2.5

RYUKYUS 0.9

TAIWAN 12.5

HONG KONG 3.7

NORTH VIETNAM 17.9

ILAND 31

CAMBODIA 6

SOUTH VIETNAM 16

PHILIPPINES 31.3

MALAYSIA 11

INDONESIA 103

OCEANIA 3.4

AUSTRALIA 11.1

NEW ZEALAND 2.6

CANADA 19.3

U.S.A. 192.1

MEXICO 39.4

CUBA 7.4

OTHER CARIBBEAN 15

CENTRAL AMERICA 13.2

VENEZUELA 8.5

COLOMBIA 16.5

BRAZIL 79.7

OTHER SOUTH AMERICA 26.1

ARGENTINA 21.3

CHILE 8.3

DESIGNED BY EDWIN O. REISCHAUER

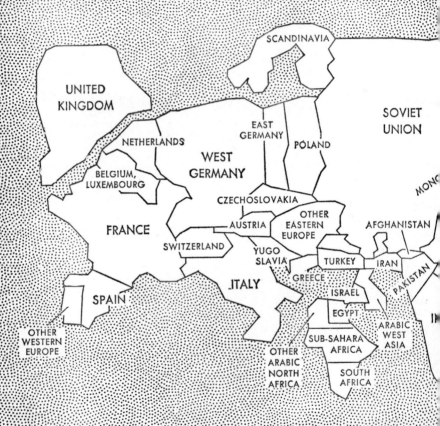

GROSS NATIONAL PRODUCT

□ REPRESENTS U.S. $1 BILLION

SCANDINAVIA

UNITED KINGDOM

SOVIET UNION

EAST GERMANY

POLAND

NETHERLANDS

WEST GERMANY

MONG

BELGIUM, LUXEMBOURG

CZECHOSLOVAKIA

FRANCE

AUSTRIA

OTHER EASTERN EUROPE

AFGHANISTAN

SWITZERLAND

YUGO SLAVIA

TURKEY

IRAN

PAKISTAN

ITALY

GREECE

ISRAEL

SPAIN

EGYPT

ARABIC WEST ASIA

OTHER WESTERN EUROPE

SUB-SAHARA AFRICA

OTHER ARABIC NORTH AFRICA

SOUTH AFRICA

DESIGNED BY EDWIN O. REISCHAUER

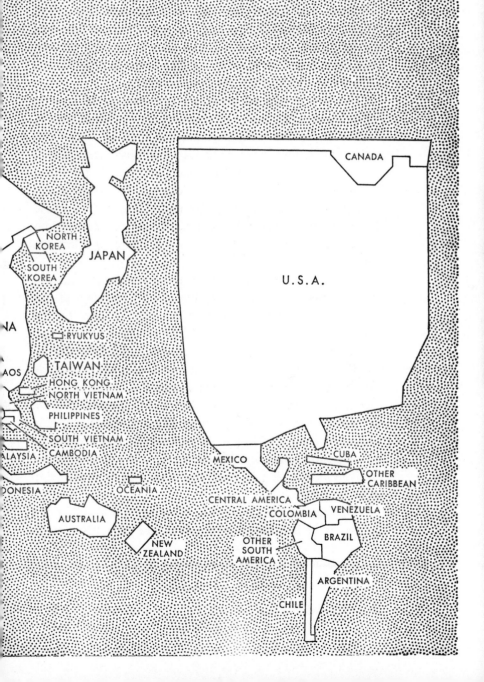

on the richer side.[1] Average per capita income is more than ten times as great in the more advanced nations as a whole than in the less advanced nations taken together, and discrepancies run higher than 50 to 1 between the richest nation, the United States, and the poorest ones. Worst of all, the contrast between rich and poor is growing greater, since the rich nations are moving ahead even in proportional terms more rapidly than the poor countries.

The less developed areas are not pockets of poverty but rather seas of poverty surrounding the islands of wealth. Poverty is for the most part accompanied by backwardness—that is, low levels of literacy and basic skills, inefficient economies, outmoded societies, and faltering political institutions. At a time of rapid change, backwardness is closely correlated with instablity and disorder. In a world that has shrunk greatly in recent years and will go on shrinking, instability in part of the world is likely to affect the whole.

In this tragic and worsening division between rich and poor nations, we see probably the greatest problem of our time—perhaps the greatest problem for the next several generations. The tensions and frictions between these two contrasting halves of the world are heightened by the instabilities of two other great fault lines that roughly coincide with the rift between North and South. All of the rich side, except for Japan, consists of countries of Occidental culture; the bulk of the other side is culturally non-Western. Again with the exception of Japan, the rich side is exclusively made up of nations that are predominantly, if not always exclusively, Caucasian in race; the other side is overwhelmingly nonwhite.

This great triple cleavage is, of course, worldwide, but a large part of it is between ourselves and Asia. Even with-

---

[1] A less rough and ready division would put a few European countries, such as Yugoslavia, Albania, Greece, and Portugal, on the poorer side of the line and Venezuela and Israel on the richer side.

out Japan, South and East Asia contain about three quarters of the population of the less developed world, while more than 40 per cent of the wealth of the advanced nations is in our hands. The size of Asia is so great and its distinctness from the other less developed regions—Latin America, the Middle East, and Africa—so marked that it is well to consider our relationship with Asia separately from these other areas, even though there are, of course, many points of similarity.

2. Our Interests in Asia

Our two maps will help us clarify the basic problem of what our interests in Asia are. Are they, for example, economic? Does Asia, by which I will mean in the rest of this chapter South and East Asia minus Japan, have much economic importance for us? I think not, at least under present conditions. Despite its huge population, Asia's low level of per capita wealth—only about one twenty-seventh that of the United States—makes its people poor customers. Nor can they supply us with much that we need. Once the rubber of Malaysia and Indonesia was important, but synthetics have reduced its value. The tin of Malaysia has some significance, as does the oil of Indonesia and various minor mineral and agricultural products, such as tungsten and hemp, but none is vital to us. The oil of the Middle East and our heavy investment in Latin America may make these areas of special economic significance to the United States, but there is no comparable American economic interest in Asia.

Quite clearly, economic matters are only a very small consideration in our relationship with Asia. Less than 3 per cent of our foreign investments are in this area. No Asian exports are crucial to us. Our trade with Asia, after aid has been subtracted from it, is much less than our trade with

Japan alone. Profits from it amount to far less than our expenditures for the area's defense. Certainly trade profits will never compensate for even a tiny fraction of the financial costs of the two wars we have fought in Asia in the past two decades.

Our maps should also make another point clear. There is little immediate menace from that part of the world to our security or vital national interests. Asia is just too weak. The total productive capacity of the whole area is much less than half that of Western Europe and less than two thirds that of the Soviet Union. But with roughly five times the population of Western Europe and seven times that of the Soviet Union, Asia uses almost all its meager production simply to keep its teeming millions alive at subsistence levels. Very little wealth is left over for purposes such as economic development, let alone threatening the vital interests of distant parts of the world.

In any case, a united Asia is of course sheer fantasy. In the early postwar years, many people apparently thought that Communism had some magic quality that could hold diverse nations together in united purpose. The history of the last decade, particularly the Sino-Soviet split, has shown how wrong this concept was. In fact, Communist countries, just because of their dogmatic beliefs, seem to find it more difficult to cooperate than do other nations, which assume, and therefore tolerate, differences of opinion. In Asia in particular, unity is difficult, through Communism or any other means. Nationalism is still too new and heady a brew to Asians for them to brook much international direction or develop any easy concert of actions.

It would be hard indeed to make any case for immediate vital American interests in Asia. Japan does much of its trade with Asia and has a lifeline of oil to the Middle East that passes through the straits of Southeast Asia. Thus it can be said to have an immediate vital interest in stability in that part of the world. One can see that Australia with its scanty population might feel apprehensive about unrest among the billion and a half people looming not far to the northwest. Since Communist China contains about half the population and production of Asia, has the largest army in the world, and is developing a small nuclear capacity, it may alarm its neighbors, even Japan, despite Japan's protective seas. China must particularly worry the Soviet Union, which shares a long and historically uneasy geographic border with it and an even more troublesome ideological border in the new "cold war" over the "true faith" of Communism. But the United States has neither geographic nor ideological borders with China; our trade with Asia is trifling in our national economy; we have no lifelines in Asia; we are far away and many times more powerful than the whole of Asia. Clearly we have no vital national interest that can be immediately and directly threatened by Asians.

Then what are our interests in Asia? Our first interest in Asia is as a major part of a now unitary world that we are trying to help toward peace, stability, and prosperity. To be sure, we are a huge, strong, and affluent nation, but the world environment inevitably has a deep effect on us too. Asia in terms of people is more than half the world. Because of the dangerous imbalance between population and wealth, and still more because of the pressure to overcome the resultant poverty and achieve greater equality with the nations of the "North," Asia is the most explosively unstable part of the world. Though far away from us, fires in Asia could lead to greater conflagrations elsewhere. The Korean War threatened to spread into a world holocaust. The Vietnam War still might. We cannot hope to have the truly peaceful world we all long for until Asia is closer to prosperity, stability, and peace.

Our second great interest is in Asia's future. Someday the Asian half of the world will probably have much more relative power than it does today. Asians are for the most part industrious people with millennia of high civilization behind them. There were long periods in the world's history when China alone far outclassed all of Europe in wealth and power and also in technological and institutional advancement. It would be rash to predict how soon or how much the present very unequal ratio of strength between Asia and the Occident will turn more in Asia's favor, but when it does, the sort of Asia that exists then will be very important to us. Will it be reasonably prosperous, stable, and healthy, or merely more explosive because it is more powerful? Will it be oriented toward world cooperation and peace or driven by deep inner tensions and desires for revenge? We have a great stake in that future Asia—far greater than in the Asia of today. We should be less concerned over what happens in Asia tomorrow than over what Asia may be twenty or fifty years from now.

We have a third interest in Asia, and this is simply our own moral imperative to help those who need help. As a people, we have for long sought to share with others what we ourselves valued. This feeling was the mainspring of the missionary movement that started a century and a half ago. It grew into a broader effort in education. Recently there has been more emphasis on economic betterment and social and political development, especially along democratic lines. Some cynics may feel that there is very little true philanthrophy in American actions abroad. I believe there is. We do genuinely wish that others might share in what we believe to be good, be it our religion, knowledge, economic well-being, or democracy. The shrinking world has in a sense brought the "slum dwellers" of Asia into our neighborhood and therefore more into our consciousness. If we did not respond in an effort to help them, the Asians would not be the only losers. We might in fact do even more harm to ourselves spiritually by betraying our own basic ideals.

In any case, however, our humanitarian activities do

tend to blend into our more self-interested efforts to build a healthier world environment for ourselves, now and in the future. The Asian half of mankind will undoubtedly have a growing influence on the well-being of the rest of us. It will become more and more difficult for the world to continue half poor and half rich, half in turmoil and half at peace. An impoverished, hungry Asia will be a continuing drain on the rest of the world. An unhappy, turbulent, and war-torn Asia will be a growing threat to all of us. We do indeed have a deep interest in the development of Asia over the years ahead. This interest is not primarily negative—to deny it to the Communists—but positive: to help it become a healthier part of the world we live in.

3. *The False Analogies*

How may Asia develop, and what can we do to help it go in a favorable direction for all of us? In trying to answer these questions, our ignorance of Asia sometimes shows through. Knowing little about its peoples and their hopes, their weaknesses, and their strengths, we have tended to visualize problems in Asia on the basis of analogies with areas we knew better, particularly Europe. Unfortunately these analogies have often proved more misleading than helpful.

In the chill of the cold war in Europe, which followed so quickly after the euphoria of victory, it was easy to think of the United States and its allies as pitted in mortal combat with a unitary Communist menace throughout the world. Communism appeared to be a single great wave beating against the dikes of freedom everywhere and threatening to breach them where they stood lowest, in Asia and the rest of the less developed world. It was assumed that once this wave had swept beyond these dikes it would never recede. The Communist triumph in China seemed to prove this. It also suggested that Asia was to be the chief battleground between Communism and the "free world." The Korean War appeared to confirm this fear.

One could envisage a future world in which unified Communism held undisputed sway from Eastern Europe and the Soviet Union through all the now less developed parts of the world. As the less developed world slowly gained in relative strength, the small remnant of advanced "free" nations would eventually be outmatched not only in population, perhaps five to one, but in wealth and power too. In desperate competition with this great Communist juggernaut, the "free world" too might then lose its freedom.

The answer to this frightening challenge seemed to be to reinforce what dikes existed against the Communist "wave of the future." In Europe a very real threat of expanding Soviet domination was met by firm action. The Communist seizure of control over an industrialized Czechoslovakia in 1948 did appreciably alter the real balance of power in Europe in favor of the Soviet Union. The threatened takeover of a strategically placed Greece through a Communist guerrilla movement could have further tipped the balance. Our response to this menace was the Truman Doctrine, enunciated in 1947, and the NATO alliance. In other words, an effective military dike was raised across Europe.

Behind this dike determined efforts were made to restore the war-torn economy of Western Europe so that the region would be less vulnerable to Communist blandishments, threats, or subversion. A massive injection of economic aid from the United States through the Marshall Plan got the countries of Europe back on their economic feet in short order, and before long they were surging ahead to new levels of prosperity. In fact, the economic terrain was built up to such a level that in time the military dike no longer seemed so important for keeping out the wave of Communism.

The story was somewhat the same in Japan, the one major industrialized nation on the other side of the world. In the early years after Japan's surrender, economic and political conditions remained so chaotic that the country seemed dangerously exposed to the Communist wave. But through our military occupation of Japan for almost seven years and then through a Mutual Security Treaty, we gave firm military defense to Japan, and, with considerable injections of economic aid, we helped restore it to economic health. Soon Japan too was racing ahead toward prosperity and gaining rapidly in political stability.

In Asia the problems were graver but, we assumed, analogous. The great Communist wave had broken through and swept over China. It broke through again in Korea— this time not in the guise of a guerrilla movement and civil war but as open aggression by massed armies. We plugged this break in the dike, but only at great cost. In Vietnam and Laos the Communist wave was slowly eating away at other soft places and threatened to spill through again in force.

Nowhere in Asia did the dikes seem strong enough or the terrain behind them high enough to avoid inundation unless we took vigorous action. Apparently we thought that what we had done with success in Europe could be repeated in Asia. We developed bilateral defense treaties with South Korea, Taiwan, and the Philippines. In 1954 we organized SEATO, named in obvious imitation of NATO. In Pakistan it overlapped wth a similarly named Middle Eastern group called CENTO (Central Treaty Organization). We had already for some years been paying for France's ineffective attempt to man the dikes in Vietnam, and in 1954 we stepped in to take its place. Meanwhile we had embarked on a massive aid program in Asia to build up the local economies and thus raise more permanent barriers to the spread of the Communist wave, as we had in Europe and Japan.

Not all of this reasoning was explicitly stated, but it certainly lay behind what we did. The analogies, however, between Asia on the one hand and Europe and Japan on the other were fundamentally false. They were based on serious misunderstandings of the situation in Asia and what we were capable of achieving there.

4. *Communism and Nationalism*

Hindsight has shown that the cold-war analysis of the situation even in Europe was not entirely accurate. Communism has proved far less monolithic and unchanging than had been assumed. Satellites have asserted their autonomy, if not full independence. Marxist economic "laws" are being abandoned for "capitalist" techniques. New cultural and intellectual currents are stirring.

The most shattering blow to Communist unity, however, has come from Asia: the Sino-Soviet split. The Humpty-Dumpty of Communist unity has fallen off the wall, and all of Marx's horses and men can never put it together again. The Russians and Chinese will probably someday wish to relax the tension between them and patch up their differences as best they can, but they can never restore what seemed to be their old monolithic unity.

I have no hesitation in saying this because back in 1954, long before the rift was apparent or had even started, I could predict it on the basis of what I knew of the fundamental attitudes of the Chinese. Commenting on the stress lines along which the "Chinese puzzle" might possibly break open, I wrote:[2]

[2] *Wanted: An Asian Policy* (New York: Knopf; 1955; Copyright by Edwin O. Reischauer), pp. 238–9.

A much more probable line of division lies between the proud Chinese and the domineering Russians, for this is a line which coincides with that sensitive frontier of contact between Asia and the West. Mao and his associates are entirely dependent on the Soviet Union for the military weapons and economic aid they must have to develop the type of China they hope to create. At the same time the Chinese can scarcely have overcome their fear of foreign domination or their resentment of the status of superiority assumed by white men during the past several generations. The Russians are unmistakably *ta-pi-tzu,* or Western "big noses," to the Chinese. In addition they are extremely dogmatic and inflexible both in theory and in practice, experienced only in clearcut relationships of authority and obedience. Even though the Chinese and Russians share the same Communist faith, it would be hard to imagine a more profoundly difficult relationship than that existing between them today.

There has been much talk about possible Titoism in China and more scornful refutation of this idea. The term is at best a poor one. It is true that Tito and Mao are the only two postwar Communist leaders who do not owe their positions largely to Russian military might, but here the comparison stops. Tito was Moscow-trained, and he is a fellow Slav as well; also, he rules over a small country not very far from the main seats of Russian power. Mao is an Asian, received no training in the Soviet Union, and is the master of a people at least twenty-five times as numerous as the Yugoslavs, living three times as far away from the main centers of Russian power. The problems of Soviet-Yugoslav relations can scarcely be compared with those inherent in the relations between the Chinese and the Russians, but only because the latter problems are so much more complex and difficult.

It seemed inevitable to me that the Chinese, the most numerous people in the world and probably the proudest, would not accept Russian leadership for long. They had

had centuries of hostile realtions with Russia. They had lost large stretches of territory once considered Chinese to Russian rule or domination—the Far Eastern Province where Vladivostok and Khabarovsk now stand, Outer Mongolia, and pieces of Central Asia. The present uneasy border runs largely through territories inhabited on both sides by Mongol- and Turkish-speaking peoples of possibly dubious allegiance to either side.

The Chinese had a deep national pride and long and bitter resentments of the Occident that made the acceptance of Russian domination extremely distasteful to them. Two such huge and different nations, even though joined by the same Communist faith, did not necessarily have mutually compatible national interests. The Communist system is based on leader-follower relationships and has no easy way of accommodating differences of opinion, even between groups in the same country, much less between nations. It assumes a single "true faith," and any departure from this is not considered just a mistaken opinion but sinful heresy. Communists have developed a whole vocabulary of abuse for other Communists whose opinions deviate in the slightest from their own. There is little possibility for agreeing to disagree.

The division of the seeming monolithic Communist system was predictable once a second great Communist power center had developed. But the Sino-Soviet rift is only the most spectacular manifestation of the inevitable Communist breakup. Yugoslavia is another, as is also the growing independence of the European satellite states. North Korea, though created through Soviet arms and defended by Chinese military power, has increasingly sought to establish its independence of both Moscow and Peking. Ho Chi Minh in Hanoi, while forced by the pressures of war to look to China and the Soviet Union for aid, has fiercely sought to maintain his independence of both. One could safely assume that the more Communism succeeds where it is entrenched and the more it spreads to other areas—if it does either—the more its original unity will disintegrate.

Thus in hindsight we see that there probably never was a single great Communist wave threatening to wash over Asia. The waters have certainly been troubled, but with a great number of different waves of change and turmoil. Communism has been but one of these and not necessarily the dominant one. Waves of Communism did sweep over certain countries and beat against the foundations of others, but, with the single exception of Korea, each of these was generated primarily within that country and did not sweep into it from outside. The Chinese Communists were basically a home-grown regime that won out on their own strength—more despite the Soviet Union than because of its aid. Early Russian domination of the movement proved disastrous, and the subsequent successes of the Chinese Communists were through methods quite at variance with those of their would-be mentors. After the war they came to power on their own steam despite the fact that Stalin had written off in his world strategy the possibility of their early victory.

In China and in almost every other country, the waves of change have not washed in from abroad but have arisen locally. Nor has Communism itself ever been the main force stirring up these waves. As we have seen, the Vietminh movement, while Communist-dominated, drew its primary strength from nationalistic yearnings for a fully independent, strong, and modernized Vietnam. The same nationalistic feelings have been a major source of strength—I would go so far as to say *the* major source of strength—of the Chinese Communists. Indeed, Communist movements have made no great impact anywhere in Asia except when they have been carried along on strong currents of nationalism.

If there is any single great wave that is sweeping across Asia, it is the nationalistic demand in every country for

 Our Asian Problem 逝 **63**

freedom from foreign domination and the right to build a strong and prosperous nation in its own way. If Communism has proved attractive to some groups, it has almost invariably been because of the assumption that it was the surest or fastest way to achieve this sort of national self-expression. Thus in Asia, nationalism is the basic driving force and Communism the technique sometimes adopted to fulfill it. While one could say that Communism has exploited nationalism, a truer description of the situation is that Communism in Asia is but one of nationalism's vehicles.

5. *The Pressures of History*

In order to understand better the relationship between nationalism and Communism in contemporary Asia, it might be well to look back briefly over recent Asian history. China maintained its lead in technology, wealth, and power over the West until about the fifteenth century. Marco Polo visited China near the end of its millennium of world leadership and was awestruck by what he saw—printing presses, which were still entirely unknown in Europe, paper money, which he considered fantastic, and dense populations and great wealth such as were undreamed of in the West. Other parts of Asia too were at least to some degree ahead of the Occident.

Thereafter the balance shifted, as Europe, with accelerating speed, forged ahead of the rest of the world in technology and in economic and military strength. In the sixteenth century, superior navigational skills and better cannon (based on the Chinese invention of gunpowder) extended European power to Asia for the first time since Alexander penetrated India. The politically more cohesive lands of East Asia fended off the growing power of the West for some time. The Japanese, already possessed of a national consciousness not unlike that of the European peoples, drove the Westerners out of their tight little islands in the early seventeenth century (except for a carefully controlled group of Dutch merchants), and the great Chinese Empire managed to hold them at arm's length for almost three centuries. The politically less cohesive countries of South and Southeast Asia, however, fell prey to expanding Occidental power, until by the latter part of the nineteenth century only islands of semi-independence, such as Thailand (then called Siam), remained free of colonial domination.

By that time Western economic and military power had grown so overwhelming that even the East Asian states could no longer withstand it. China, then sinking into one of its periodic dynastic declines, was forced in 1842 to accept the first of a series of unequal treaties that progressively deprived it of some of its sovereign rights and also key bits of territory. Japan, faced with the same prospect, erupted into violent counteraction.

In 1853–4 Commodore Perry of the United States demonstrated to the Japanese through superior naval power that Occidentals now could beat down their closed doors, as had happened in China, if these doors were not voluntarily opened. The Japanese, while cautiously opening their doors, busily set about building for themselves the same sort of economic and military power that the West was using to menace their independence. They were aided in this by several factors. They already constituted an extraordinarily homogeneous nation-state. While superficially divided into a number of semi-autonomous feudal units, they had derived from a long feudal experience, much like that of Europe, more complicated and in many ways more advanced economic, social, and political institutions than existed elsewhere in Asia and a kind of diversity that allowed for a rich variety of responses. Their feudal society also seems to have produced a sort of goal-oriented, as opposed to status-oriented, ethical system, reminiscent of the so-called "Protestant ethic" of the West. In any case, the Japanese, like Occidentals, had strong entrepreneurial drives. Moreover, their history as a rather remote cultural daughter of China—much as the nations of North Europe had been cultural offshoots of Mediterranean civilization—had made them very conscious of the possibility of learning useful things from abroad.

Thus for a variety of reasons the Japanese were able to throw themselves with determination and amazing success into the task of learning the technical skills of the West and modernizing their nation. By the end of the nineteenth century Japan had already got rid of the unequal treaties the Western nations had imposed; in 1904–5 it defeated one of the greatest of them, Russia, in a major war; and, by the end of the First World War, it had won recognition as one of the five great powers of the world. The Japanese had made a superbly successful nationalistic response to the Western challenge, though in their subsequent excesses of nationalism they were to plunge Japan and the rest of East Asia into the tragedy of the Second World War.

The story in China was far different. Fear and resentment of foreign domination was as great there as in Japan, but China reacted less successfully. It was a huge, centralized empire but was partially paralyzed by dynastic decay. China's history tends to fall into dynastic cycles—a period of rising power under a new imperial line, then a period of stagnation as increasing luxury at court outruns tax resources and government begins to suffer from hardening of the bureaucratic arteries, and finally a period of growing disruption and eventual collapse. In the middle of the nineteenth century, China was entering the third stage. Moreover, the age-old assumption that China was the unique land of civilization, surrounded by lesser barbarian breeds who participated in civilization only to the extent that they admitted China's cultural and political suzerainty, made it difficult for the Chinese to follow the Japanese course of utilizing the superior technology of the West to fend off the encroachments of the West.

China was repeatedly convulsed by movements to drive out the foreigners or to reform the government and modernize the country, but none succeeded. The Taiping Rebellion swept the land from 1850 to 1864 but finally collapsed. Reform movements in the 1880's and 1890's ended in frustration. The violently anti-Western Boxer Uprising disrupted North China in 1900. In 1911–12 the old empire was overthrown, but the Republic that succeeded it fell apart into a number of warlord domains. The Kuomintang, reorganized along Russian Communist lines, drove northward from Canton in late 1926 under the military leadership of Chiang Kai-shek and gave great promise for a while of unifying the country and achieving national rehabilitation. Before Chiang had established his control over the whole country, however, the Japanese militarists, alarmed by the possible challenge to their interests of a strong China, moved to the attack. They first seized Manchuria in 1931 and then in 1937 started the war in China that finally grew into the Pacific half of the Second World War.

Meanwhile the Communists under Mao Tse-tung were gradually becoming the spearhead of a new drive for national unity and strength. They had been allied with the Kuomintang from 1923 to 1926, but Chiang had turned on them the next year. After a long period of near extinction, the war with Japan presented them with an opportunity to extend their power through successful guerrilla activities from their base in northwest China. By the latter stages of the Second World War they were clearly a well-organized, rising force, and Chiang's Kuomintang, driven by the Japanese from its bases of power in the coastal cities and pushed into the backward areas of southwestern China, was a seriously disrupted and fading regime that seemed no longer to hold out much promise for national regeneration.

It is not surprising that increasing numbers of Chinese, smarting from a century of national humiliation at the hands of outside "barbarians," looked to the Communists rather than to the Kuomintang as the best hope for a strong and self-respecting China. The Communists thus swept to victory, not so much because of the appeal of international Communism or its doctrines of class conflict, but because they seemed best able to build an entirely independent, strong, and modernized China.

The story in South Asia is different again, but the moral is the same. There was at first less reaction against Western domination in the ethnically more diverse and politically less cohesive lands to the south than there had been in East Asia. The Occidentals seemed like just one more layer of rulers in these multilayered societies. Western education, however, brought to these lands concepts of nationalism that in time made at least the educated classes restive. The Japanese victory over Russia in 1904–5 then sent a tremor of hope through them. If the Japanese could defy Western domination, why could not other Asians?

The Second World War marks the great watershed in modern Asian history. The Japanese had no intention of freeing their own colonies in Korea and Taiwan, and the "independent" Asian regimes they set up in the countries they conquered were designed to be mere satellites in Japan's so-called "Greater East Asia Co-Prosperity Sphere." The ease with which Japan overran the Western colonial territories of Southeast Asia, however, showed that Occidental rule there was only a thin and fragile shell. The war also brought Japan's more firmly held empire down in ruin. Moreover, the successes of the Chinese Communists in guerrilla warfare against the Japanese in North China demonstrated that, in a less developed country, a nationalistically aroused and organized peasantry could frustrate efforts at control by a vastly superior foreign army. Under these changed circumstances, the small nationalistic movements, which had been stirring ineffectually against colonial domination in Asia, soon became an irresistible force that swept away for all time the colonial empires of the past.

6. *The Dynamics of Change*

The empires are now gone, but Asians are still basically reacting against a century or more of colonial or semi-colonial domination by the West and against their own poverty, backwardness, and relative impotence, which they tend to attribute to this domination by outsiders. They are determined to break free from this humiliating past. They will brook no form of control or undue influence from abroad and are determined to sweep away anything at home that seems to stand in the way of their own progress toward affluence and strength. They are almost by definition against the status quo and for change. "Revolution" rather than "defense" is the operational word.

Almost all Asians perceive the modern nation-state as the unit through which they can best achieve independence, regeneration and international self-respect. Even in areas where political unity has been rare in the past, they have developed the belief in the overriding importance of the national grouping and the deep emotional attachment to it that we call nationalism. They expect it to have the same magic for them that it has had for the West. This has been true even in countries like India and Pakistan, where religion has been the major unifying factor and nationalism has not been backed up by any unity of language.

Nationalism, of course, has its destructve as well as its constructive aspects. However helpful it has been to nation-building, it has also been the cause of countless wars and innumerable senseless frictions between countries. The peoples of the more advanced nations, which have long been nationalistic, are now beginning to see how dangerous nationalism can be. In the countries of Western Europe as well as in the United States and Japan, people are trying to look beyond nationalism to a more tolerant internationalism, in which patriotism to one's own national unit can be incorporated into a broader loyalty to humanity and civilization as a whole.

We might hope, therefore, that Asians, seeing our own sad record of nationalistic excesses, will somehow skip this phase of development and go straight to internationalism. This, however, seems to me a vain hope. In the modern world, nation-states seem to be indispensable building blocks for economic progress and institutional modernization. How can we expect Asians to develop enough enthusiasm to create these apparently necessary basic units of organization without at the same time producing some of the nationalistic frictions—possibly even wars—which the advanced nations experienced in such number during their own modernization as national units? Certainly there are plenty of signs of this already in Asia, as in the rivalry between India and Pakistan and the animosities between Cambodia and its neighbors. We should be tolerant and understanding, not expecting more of Asians than we were capable of ourselves at a comparable stage in our national development. We can only hope that the example of history, together with the stronger worldwide sense of an international order that exists today, will help Asian countries avoid some of the destructive aspects of nationalism.

Actually nationalism has performed well for Asians. It did sweep away the colonial empires of the past. A Pakistan divided into two geographically distant parts and an India made up of a welter of linguistic groups have held together remarkably well, despite a number of serious trials. Indonesia, which consists merely of the island territories the Dutch through historical accident had come to rule, has been made into a nation-state. For all his faults,

Sukarno, through little more than nationalistic ardor, succeeded in forging a nation where none had ever existed before. The smaller and more homogeneous political units have also drawn unprecedented strength from nationalism. Of course, nationalism faces greater hurdles in the form of differing languages, ethnic groups, and religions within many Asian countries than it did in Japan or in most Western lands, but this makes it, in a sense, all the more important to Asians as a unifying force.

Most Asians have also realzed that to build strong nations they must first have a great deal of economic development. Rapid industrialization has usually been seen as the panacea for this. After initial failures, however, there has been a growing realization that, in these still largely rural lands, agricultural growth must accompany, if not precede, any significant degree of industrialization.

There has been less agreement in Asia over the best means to achieve national consolidation and economic progress. The free societies and political democracy of the West have proved attractive to most Asians who know about them. I might explain that by democracy I, of course, mean the political system of rule through parliamentary institutions, based on free elections, based in turn on freedom of expression and well-established civil rights. It may seem strange that I need to make this explanation, but the term "democracy" is so much misused these days that it may be wise to define it. Frequently it is used to denote egalitarian societies or socialist economies, and it has been appropriated by almost all dictatorial governments that profess to rule in behalf of the people. To operate successfully in the modern day, a democracy naturally requires a considerable degree of egalitarianism in society, and it may choose to try to create a socialist economic system, as several democracies have done. Democracy itself, however, if it is to be used as anything more than an emotional color term, should be limited to its traditional meaning of a specific type of political system, of which Communist and other one-party or individual dictatorships are the virtual antithesis.

Democracy in this sense, as I have said, has had and continues to have a broad appeal in Asia. For example, in Japan there was a mounting popular demand for democracy from the 1870's on. During the next half century, the Japanese, despite the opposition of strong elements in their authoritarian government, repeated in foreshortened form much of the history of the development of democracy in Western Europe. This remarkable achievement was temporarily eclipsed by militarism in the 1930's and 1940's, but after the war, with some assistance from the American occupation forces, Japan's home-grown democracy blossomed into a successful and stable system of parliamentary government. The Chinese after the Republican Revolution of 1911–12 also tried to develop a democracy but, finding themselves unprepared for it, passed on to warlordism and then to party dictatorship, first by the Kuomintang and then by the Communists. Almost all the formerly colonial lands of Asia launched their new independent careers as would-be democracies. A few, such as India, Ceylon, the Philippines, and Malaysia, still maintain democratc institutions, but most of the rest, finding them hard to operate, have drifted to military dictatorships. Even among the Communist or military dictatorships of Asia, however, the attractiveness of the democratic ideal is usually recognized through lip service paid to the word "democracy" itself.

We should not be surprised at the limited success democracy has had in Asia. The record there, as elsewhere in the less developed world, shows that free public debate, true popular elections, and parliamentary rule are political techniques that are not easy to institute or maintain in backward areas. This is particularly true today when the assumption is that any democratic system must be based from the start on universal suffrage. Both in the West and in Japan, the early steps in democracy were taken at a time when limitations of the electorate by wealth or education were acceptable, but such limitations are not considered tolerable any more. Economic expectations also run far higher today, and the pace of change is much faster. Fledgling democracies find it difficult to cope with either.

Thus a new democracy today must start by running, not walking, as we and the Japanese did at first in our progress toward democracy. But how many less developed countries have the skills for this? For a country to operate successfully a fullscale, modern democratic system, it must have a public with a considerable degree of political experience, it must have relatively high levels of education, and it must have a degree of economic well-being that permits a good part of the citizenry to look beyond the problem of their next few meals. It would be impossble to determine just what the minimum requirements are, and they probably vary from country to country, depending on various other factors. But in any case they seem to be as yet unattained in most Asian lands. It is not surprising that some countries have turned from unsuccessful experiments in democracy to other more easily operated forms of governments, such as Communism and military dictatorship.

Another reason why democracy has difficulty in taking root in Asia is that the traditional societies tend to be elitist, as in the caste system of India or the domination of a scholar-gentry-bureaucrat class in Confucian China. The colonial regimes aggravated the situation by training a new elite in the language of the colonial masters, separating them in thinking and sometimes in way of life from the masses. Thus, because of ancient precedent and more recent colonial experience, many Asian countries have a society that lends itself more to a leader-follower type of dictatorial system than to democracy.

This sort of elitism also may influence Asian choices of methods to achieve economic progress and industrialization.

It is not unnatural for elitist leaders to picture themselves at the head of a socialistically inclined state, shaping the economic future for the apathetic and uneducated peasants, rather than waiting for private initiative to appear in adequate measure from among the slow-moving masses. This, however, is by no means the only reason why Asians have tended to show strong predilections for a socialist system rather than a freer or "mixed" economy.

During the 1920's and 1930's, when many of Asia's postwar leaders were studying in the West, Marxist claims of the superiority of a planned, state-controlled economy over "capitalism" were strong in many intellectual circles in Europe. Communism in particular appealed to Asian students because it purported to explain their major woes and show how these could be overcome. According to Communist theory, the imperialism that had robbed Asians of their political freedom was the inevitable product of the capitalistic system entering on its death throes, and capitalistic exploitation of Asia accounted for Asian poverty and social backwardness. A Communist "dictatorship of the proletariat" would make it possible for the less developed countries to leap over the whole "bourgeois" stage of historical development and move ahead of their erstwhile "oppressors." Thus, if capitalism were expunged, the road apparently would be opened to independence and to economic growth.

As a matter of historical fact, these propositions were probably more wrong than right, but they coincided with natural Asian prejudices. The colonial powers were indeed capitalistic, and therefore capitalism could be easily identified with the evil past that Asians wished to leave behind them. And once the political control of the West was broken, the chief remaining danger seemed to be continued economic bondage through foreign business interests. It appeared all too possible that the rich countries of the West might maintain their domination over the poor lands of Asia through covert economic means, even when giving up overt political control.

In addition, conditions in most Asian lands did not seem well suited to a program of rapid growth through a free economy. There was little surplus wealth available for economic investment; living standards were so low that any increase in wealth was likely to be eaten up by increases in consumption; and thus it seemed that, if much capital were to be invested in industrialization, the government would have to squeeze the money out of the people and control the investment process. Moreover, most Asian countries lacked the highly developed managerial skills in government and business that the Japanese already possessed in the nineteenth century, and the resultant political and economic instability discouraged what entrepreneurial skills their peoples may have possessed. Private capital tended to continue to go into investment in land or into commercial activities that promised a rapid turnover, but not into long-range industrial investment. In many Asian lands, therefore, local private entrepreneurship seemed too slow and uncertain a force to depend on for the development of the economy.

Since democracy is so hard to operate in Asia and socialist doctrines have more natural appeal than "capitalism," it is not surprising that some Asian leaders have embraced Communism as the best way to get their countries on their feet, for it combines simple, dictatorial methods of government with a socialized economy. Even in the West after the Russian Revolution, many people came to believe that Communist techniques were the quickest and best way to industrialize and modernize a country. During the two decades between the First and Second World Wars, some of the future leaders of Asia, such as Chou En-lai of China and Ho Chi Minh, studied in the West and absorbed these ideas. Others, like Mao Tse-tung, picked them up at home. Their countries, they felt, needed to smash the status quo through revolution. Communism seemed to them to represent the most advanced form of the stronger technology of the West and the best means by which to effect rapid change in their own countries. But their basic goal was not to establish a Communist system for itself but to achieve through it national independence and regeneration.

The important point is that Asian leaders, whether Communist, socialist, democratic, elitist, or whatever, have usually regarded these various approaches as merely means to an end—the end of building independent, self-respecting, strong, and prosperous nations. Communism has had some advantages in the competition between the several means to this nationalistic end. The guerrilla war techniques Asian Communists have developed constitute a very effective way to seize power in a less developed country. Their methods of political indoctrination have proved to be extremely efficient in gaining popular support. When they have tailored their social and economic theories to fit strong popular desires, as in the distribution of land to tenant cultivators, they have seized on powerful levers of control.

Communism, however, also suffers from serious handicaps in Asia. Marxism was based on an analysis of European industrialized societies of the nineteenth century, not on pre-industrial Asian lands of the twentieth. Its theories fit very poorly the realities of Asia. Much of its dogma is almost meaningless. Its economic doctrines are bad guides. When Communists go beyond "land reform" to the building of peasant communes, they not only irritate the peasants by taking away their land once more but seriously impair agricultural production, which still accounts for the bulk of the economy in most Asian lands. The well-known Communist "brown thumb" in agriculture is even more of a disaster for Asia than it is for Europe.

Communism's antireligious stand is also a strong drawback in the more religiously oriented lands of Asia, such as Hindu India; Buddhist Ceylon, Burma, Thailand and

Cambodia; and Moslem Pakistan, Indonesia, and Malaysia. But its greatest handicap, at least in countries where it has not already won out, is its internationalism. The suspicion that a Communist party might be dominated by Peking or Moscow is sometimes its Achilles heel. Indonesia turned dramatically against Communism in the autumn of 1965 partly because of religious fears of the Communists but much more because of nationalistic resentment of the Communists' ties with China.

In conclusion, we see that the waves of change sweeping Asia are not a single great Communist wave or a series of nationalistically divided Communist waves. They are a variety of convulsive efforts to get away from the humiliations of the past and move with speed toward a more self-respecting future. Some of these attempts may have a Communist coloration, but this is only one of many forms they make take.

In fact, in many areas Communism is beginning to look like the wave of the past. Growing experience in trying to deal with economic problems is also making many Asians less enthusiastic about socialism and more pragmatic and flexible in their economic policies. They are getting past the emotionalism and oversimplifications of ideology and facing up to the complexities of reality. The leadership in Pakistan presents a notable example of this change. Since the debacle of Sukarno-ism, the youth of Indonesia also shows a similar disenchantment with ideology. Even the psychological pressures built up by colonialism are beginning to sink slowly into history in some parts of Asia. Thus bit by bit efforts at change are becoming more constructive and more realistic.

We should note, however, that whether destructive or constructive, none of the efforts at change in Asia has as yet been very successful in creating the prosperity, strength, and prestige that Asian countries seek. All have experienced failures and face frustrations of one sort or another. Not the least of these failures and frustrations have been experienced by Communist China. None of the countries of Asia is as yet very stable. All seem subject to rapid and upsetting changes. Expectations outpace the realities of growth, leading to bitter disappointment and sometimes unrest. The recent Cultural Revolution and Red Guard movements in China show that this is as true there as in the non-Communist countries. The colonial past may have been destroyed, but no new tolerable status quo has been achieved. Asians continue to demand, if not revolution, at least revolutionary change.

7. *The Military Threat*

On the basis of this brief analysis of recent Asian history and the dynamics of change there, let us take another look at the analogies drawn between our problems in Asia and those we faced in Europe and Japan. If we do this, we will see how very misleading these analogies have been. On almost every major point, the situation was fundamentally different.

In the early postwar years, Soviet military power, already spread over all Eastern Europe, seemed a real menace to the war-ravaged lands of Western Europe. There was a genuine nationalistic fear of the apparently unitary threat of the Russian-dominated Communist movement. Being racially akin to us and sharing a common cultural heritage, the people of Western Europe welcomed us as overseas "cousins" come to their aid. Since their countries all had long histories as nations and were for the most part democratically organized and institutionally sound, they offered firm political terrain for whatever defense lines we wished to construct with them. Already for the most part industrialized, technologically advanced, and economically modernized, they needed only a limited amount of time and aid to restore their economies and start moving ahead again. Thus they offered solid political, economic, and psychological foundations for our military and economic efforts in their behalf. With their wholehearted cooperation, our policies proved spectacularly successful, and the rapid restoration of strong, secure and healthy nations in Western Europe soon tipped the world balance of power quite decisively in favor of our interests.

Not a single sentence or clause in the preceding paragraph finds a parallel in much of postwar Asia. For most Asians the enemy was not Soviet military might or later the rising power of Communist China so much as the past colonial or semicolonial domination of the West. It was Occidental countries like the United States and coming like us by sea that raised their deepest fears. Insofar as they had adopted Marxist concepts—and many had—they regarded the capitalism that we seemed to champion as the chief continung threat of domination from the West and looked to socialism, the economic system the Russians proclaimed, as their main hope for progress. We did not seem either racially or culturally like friendly "cousins" but rather a new and bigger form of the sort of Western nation that had dominated them in the past. Both by our appearances and our economic system we were frighteningly reminiscent of the humiliating past they were trying to escape.

I do not mean to suggest that most Asians viewed us with open hostility at the end of the war. Quite the contrary. There was great respect and admiration for us almost everywhere. We had proved successful in war, smashing the Japanese hold on East Asia and opening the way to independence in many Asian countries. We alone had vast economic resources undamaged by war and were thus the chief potential source of outside help. Despite our lack of experience in international leadership, particularly in Asia, we plunged with good will and vigor into the task of making a better postwar world. All this was realized by many

Asians, but they nonetheless looked at us through different eyes from those of Europeans.

The military situation in Asia was also very different from that in Europe. South Korea was more an exception than the rule. For Koreans, the Japanese rather than Westerners represented the colonial past. Russian military power, as in Eastern Europe, lay behind the establishment of a Communist regime in North Korea. We had occupied the South at the end of the war and had started it on its road to independence. The Korean War resulted from open aggression by the North, rather than from internal subversion or guerrilla fighting, and was fought as a conventional war of the sort in which our military power is effective. Korea is a more homogeneous national unit than are most of the countries of South Asia, and the Russian-imposed Communist regime of the North, its cruelty during the war, and the Chinese Communist intervention in the war united South Koreans in bitter hatred of Communism. The parallels here with Europe were marked.

In China, however, the story was far different. There was no foreign intervention except for the brief Russian entry into Manchuria and our temporary military control of the major coastal cities. China was disrupted by a wholly indigenous civil war, and victory went to the side that controlled the smaller and poorer part of the country and population and had the smaller forces and inferior weapons, but had the stronger will to fight and greater popular support. A massive flow of dollars, goods, and weapons from us to Chiang's government could not save it. Even if we had intervened directly ourselves—which in any case the postwar mood of the American people made politically out of the question—we probably could have done no more than delay Chiang's defeat. If we had entered the war ourselves, the vast terrain and population of China and the skills at guerrilla warfare of the Chinese Communists would have multiplied many times over for us the frustrations we have experienced in the Vietnam War. Only when the Kuomintang withdrew to Taiwan did it manage to stabilize its now much shrunken position. Here the higher economic and institutional foundations built up during Japanese colonial rule gave it firmer footing, and the Taiwan Straits, with an assist from American naval power, gave it military protection, though minor military clashes continue with the Communist mainland.

In the twenty-two years of unrest and warfare in Vietnam the contest has been between Vietnamese or against assorted foreigners from the "free world"—primarily French and Americans. Laos has been wracked by complex internal strife, supported on the one side by Communist North Vietnam and on the other by us. Indonesia experienced an anticolonial war against the Dutch and then various internal uprisings, revolutions, and *coups d'état.* The Philippines and Malaysia (then called Malaya) faced protracted insurgency movements mounted by local Communists, and Malaysia underwent for a while an inept and halfhearted attack by Indonesia. Thailand faces a small insurgency movement in its northeastern corner and desultory troubles in the extreme south. Burma has been torn by two indigenous Communist movements and dissidence on the part of various minority groups. India has faced small-scale uprisings of minority groups and more serious border wars with Pakistan and China.

This sorry record of strife and turmoil contrasts sharply with the postwar history of Western Europe. And no Chinese, much less Soviet, troops have been involved in all this fighting, except for Korea and the border war between China and India in 1962. In regard to these two exceptions, it is worth noting how the fighting looked from the Chinese point of view. They entered the Korean War only after our armies had approached their Manchurian border with North Korea and after they had given us clear warnings against doing this. Remembering the history of Japanese aggression against China by way of Korea and Manchuria, they seemed to have regarded our advance toward Manchuria as a direct threat to their security and decided to come out to meet us in self-defense. In the Sino-Indian War, the Chinese may have wished to embarrass the Soviet Union, but their interest with regard to India was only to "correct" the border in line with their ideas of where it belonged and to humble the Indians, not to try to control any part of India proper or force Communism on it. In fact, the war proved to be a great blow to the whole Communist movement in India. The Vietnam War is sometimes spoken of as if it were an example of Chinese military aggression, but, at the time of this writing, China had sent only some 40,000 noncombatant engineers into North Vietnam, which is less than a tenth as many men as the fighting forces we have sent halfway around the world to South Vietnam.

Without doubt the Chinese Communists, and also probably the Soviets, have done what they could to promote Communist movements and stir up strife in all parts of Asia. But, except in Korea, their means have not been by the sort of open aggression against which military defense lines can be erected. Communist movements in Asia, whether or not they have been aided and abetted by China or the Soviet Union, have thrived primarily on local discontent. The most dangerous have turned into guerrilla-type insurgences. The answer to these usually seems as much economic and political as military. The Communist insurgency in the Philippines dwindled away when President Magsaysay backed up his military efforts with economic and political countermeasures and the promise of a better day, and it has revived recently under his less competent and less inspiring successors.

The record of trying to hold military defense lines against Communism has also not been an encouraging one in Asia, except for the unique case of Korea. External military power provided by the British did stamp out a Communist guerrilla movement in Malaya, but the insurgency was numerically very small, and its suppression took many years of great effort. In China massive military aid on our part proved fruitless. Our weapons and supplies passed so rapidly into the hands of the Communists that we became a major source of supply for them. In Laos over the years, a flow of aid and support that is totally disproportionate to the size and importance of this extremely backward land of only two and a half million people has not brought peace or security to it. We have already seen how little has been achieved with our tremendous military investment in Vietnam.

It is not surprising that certain precariously balanced countries, notably Cambodia and Burma, have felt that they could better defend themselves against internal Communist subversion or external Communist pressure by staying strictly away, not only from our military protection, but even from our economic aid. Indonesia also is an interesting case in point. A dangerously mounting threat on the part of a strong indigenous Communist party was ruthlessly crushed in the early autumn of 1965 at a time when Indonesia had broken all but the thinnest diplomatic ties with us.

Some people argue that, without our military stand in Vietnam, the Indonesians would not have mustered the courage to crush the Communist movement in their country. I do not think that the record of the early hours of the crucial clash bears this out. The generals who destroyed the Communists were literally fighting for their lives against an attempted Communist coup and obviously were not stopping to evaluate the influence of the military situation in Vietnam on their long-range prospects. I would agree that if American naval power, which can give an island country like Indonesia security from foreign aggression, had not been present in the Western Pacific and if American economic aid in the past and more specifically our training programs for the Indonesian military had not helped strengthen counterweights to the Communist movement, the 1965 blowup in

Indonesia might have come out quite differently. On the other hand, one of the reasons why the Indonesians crushed the Communists with such thoroughness may have been just because there was at that time no important American presence in Indonesia and therefore Chinese influence over the local Communists loomed all the more as the greatest threat of outside domination.

The Indonesian case may be a debatable one, but when we stop to analyze the situation in Asia as a whole, it is not surprising that our great military power is relatively ineffective in the area. The countries there are economically backward and politically weak. In such lands, guerrilla wars are easy to mount and extremely difficult to suppress. These, rather than external aggression, are the real threat. Our military power is not geared for guerrilla warfare. As in Vietnam, we turn into an elephant vainly trying to combat gnats. When we shift to counter-guerrilla techniques, we give up much of our great technological superiority and meet Asians more on the man-to-man level in which we are numerically at a serious disadvantage and have the further disability of being in unfamiliar territory. Experts have estimated that a 10 to 1 superiority in manpower is necessary to stamp out a guerrilla movement. Vietnam has shown all too clearly the absurdity of the concept that we can play the role of policeman for all Asia.

In addition, our very presence in a war-torn Asian country tends to work against the cause we are supporting. For one thing, our huge military machine, with its vast support mechanisms, is likely to become an almost unbearable weight on the local economy, proving as disruptive of society as it may be helpful militarily. We have seen this in the Korean War and more recently and more seriously in Vietnam. We are like the man who seeks to help his neighbor weed his garden by bringing in a bulldozer. Worse still is the fact that we appear in Asian eyes so much like the colonial masters of the past that we help make those who oppose us seem to be the "real" nationalists and those whom we support the "running dogs" of neo-imperialism. Thus unlike Europe, where our military and economic assistance was effective and almost pure gain for those we sought to help, in Asia our military power is sharply reduced in effectiveness and can have seriously adverse economic and political effects.

8. Economic Development

Containment in Europe was in a sense a temporary strategy, designed to give Western Europe time to recover its economic strength and political stability. This was quickly achieved, and the tensions and burdens of the containment policy then started to decline. In Asia quick economic recovery is impossible—basically because it is not a question of "recovery." Unlike the European countries or Japan, which were restoring their war-torn but already modernized and industrialized economies, Asian nations have to go through the much slower process of economic modernization and industrialization. European and Japanese recovery took only a few years, but growth of the sort Asia needs may require as many decades or even generations.

All too commonly, population growth eats up most of the slow gain in production. In the West and Japan the early stages of economic modernization took place before modern hygiene and medicine had brought death rates as far down as they are today, and by the time death rates had greatly declined, these countries had developed the sort of urban, industrialized societies that tend to have low birth rates. Thus, for example, population growth in Japan never reached even 2 per cent a year and recently has fallen below 1 per cent. In the Occident, moreover, new lands in the Western Hemisphere and elsewhere permitted the emigration of excess population.

In the less developed countries of today, however, advances in hygiene, together with modern transportation facilities that have virtually eliminated local famines, have brought death rates down at a time when birth rates have remained at the high levels typical of pre-industrialized societies, and there is no place to which excess population can escape. As a consequence, throughout the less developed world, mouths to be fed are increasing at the rate of 2 to 3.5 per cent a year. Production, however, is rarely increasing at more than 6 per cent and in some cases is stationary or even falling. Net rates of growth in production over population probably average no better than 1 or 2 per cent per year, which is below the average for the advanced nations. Thus the gap between them is widening not just in absolute terms but in percentages as well.

Neither Americans nor Asians seemed to understand these problems fully in the early postwar years, and as a consequence there has been a great deal of disillusionment over the slow rate of economic progress in Asia. The disappointment has been worst, of course, among Asians themselves, because it is their lives and their dreams that are affected. Even among Americans, however, there has developed a corrosive sense of frustration or even betrayal over Asia's very modest economic gains despite our massive efforts at aid. Unrealistic expectations that aid to Asian countries could achieve quick results comparable to those of the Marshall Plan in Europe have turned sometimes to deep skepticism about the utility of giving any aid to Asia. Such attitudes, paralleling as they do the serious frustrations of the war in Vietnam, could contribute to the swing toward isolationism I have discussed above.

The real experts in economic development, both in Asia

and the United States, never equated Asian economic growth with European recovery, but I suspect that they had in the back of their minds another more plausible, but equally misleading, analogy. This was with Japan, which had so spectacularly modernized and industrialized its economy in the second half of the nineteenth century and the early twentieth century.

Japan had been able to do this in part because it was already a firm national unit and was nationalistically aroused against the foreign menace. It therefore seemed plausible that, now that the other Asian peoples were organizing into independent national units and were stirred by nationalistic sentiments, they would be able to do the same, only faster. Just as Japan, provided with a model of industrialization in the West, was apparently able to cut corners in industrializing, the newer nations of Asia, benefiting from our now more advanced understanding of economic modernization, could cut even more corners. Moreover, Japan had had no free foreign aid, but rather had been forced to pay high rates of interest for capital investments and high prices for the skills it imported, since it was then considered a poor economic risk and an undesirable place to live. Now that both capital and skills could be supplied from abroad either gratis or at specially low rates, economic advance could be much faster than it had been in the case of Japan.

All this reasoning was correct as far as it went, but it overlooked certain key points. The technological gap between Japan and the West was much less a century ago than that between most of Asia and the West today. We have moved far beyond where we were then, and Japan even at that time was in many respects ahead of many Asian countries today. It was a much more solid national entity than most. There was no dangerous cultural gap between the leadership and the masses. There was a strong tradition of hard work. There were firm habits of thrift that find few parallels in Asia or anywhere else in the world. There was a pervasive desire for education among the people. Literacy rates, which may have been around 40 per cent for men and 10 to 15 per cent for women, were comparable to those of the West at that time and well ahead of many Asian countries even today. The rural economy was more advanced in many important respects than that of much of contemporary Asia, and agricultural production responded to the opening of international trade after 1860 by rapid and prolonged growth. There was a wealth of the sort of individual entrepreneurial initiative that is so notably lacking in much of Asia.

Even with these advantages, Japan experienced a period of serious instability and internal strife between 1863 and 1877, did not get a sound administrative and financial basis for modernization until the middle 1880's, and did not begin any very great industrial growth until the late 1880's and 1890's. Thereafter its economic history paralleled that of the West, though at accelerated speed. In quicker sequence it ran through the steps of success in textiles and light industries, then heavy industries, and then on into chemicals, sophisticated machinery, and electronics.

The Japanese case would suggest that there are really no shortcuts to economic modernization—only a possibility of speeding up the process of industrialization when the environment is favorable. It also suggests that certain prerequisites—strong national solidarity, administrative and financial stability, good work habits, a strong propensity to save, high literacy, capacities for sustained agricultural growth, entrepreneurial skills, and the like—may be necessary before any great economic modernization is possible. It may take considerable time before enough of these characteristics have been developed in some Asian countries to permit them to move ahead rapidly with industrialization. Clearly if our policies of economic aid in Asia are to be meaningful, they should be aimed, not at quick results, as in postwar Europe, but at a process of development over many decades.

9. *The Status Quo*

Another great difference between Asia and Europe is that in the latter what was desired was defense, recovery, and then evolutionary progress, while in Asia prevailing national sentiments demand revolutionary change. Neither defense nor recovery seems to Asians to be the real need. There is nothing satisfactory to be recovered; the status quo is to be changed, not defended. Evolutionary progress from colonialism toward independence was not enough. It had to be achieved by revolutionary change—sometimes by actual revolutions. Economic and social progress cannot be left to presumably slow evolutionary processes but must be achieved by forced marches. As in most of the less developed world and even in the less advanced of the industrialized nations, revolution is virtually equated with progress. It is glorified as almost the ultimate good.

A more sober reading of history would probably show that much more progress has been achieved in the world by evolution than by revolution. The most advanced countries tend to be those which have had the fewest revolutionary changes. Revolution has figured little in the modern history of the English-speaking nations and even then only at relatively early stages in the modernization process. It also figures very little in the history of the Scandanavians, the Swiss, or the Dutch. It plays more of a role, but still not the major part, in the modernization of France, which institutionally fell behind in the eighteenth century, and with the Germans, Japanese, and Italians, who were comparatively late starters in modernization.

In a sense, revolution can be regarded as the sign of

failure at evolutionary progress. Its destructiveness is the high price paid for this failure, but it sometimes is necessary to pay this price if progress is to be made at all. It is sometimes needed to remove barriers to growth, to break rigidly frozen institutions, to remove the dead hand of the past. We who have forged far ahead through evolutionary progress should be tolerant of the impatience of those who have fallen behind because of the failure of their societies to make adequate advances in this way. We should understand their belief in the need for revolutionary change. We should not expect them to be as satisfied as we are with the status quo or call on them to place the same stress we do on its defense.

Unfortunately the analogy with Europe led us to bring to our Asian problems the same emphasis on defense and the status quo that had proved successful in dealing with the problems of Europe. As a result, we often found ourselves allied primarily with those elements in Asia most interested in preserving the status quo or defending their particular interests. Sometimes these were whole national or seminational units, like South Korea or the Chinese Nationalist regime on Taiwan, which because of a particular historical experience viewed the Communist menace in much the same way we did. But in other cases it was the remnants of colonialism, like the French in Vietnam, or special privileged groups that looked upon any change as inimical to their prerogatives. Commonly it was a political regime that, having failed in its efforts to move forward, was desperately clinging to power in the face of mounting attacks by those demanding more change. Thus we tended to become identified with the domestic status quo, which was generally felt to be intolerable. We got stuck in close embrace with regimes that even we could recognize were not adequate to meet the needs for change in Asia. This was the story with Syngman Rhee in Korea and with Diem in Vietnam.

Our well-meaning efforts to help defend and aid nations

thus can be easily misinterpreted as an attempt to stop change and to perpetuate an unsatisfactory status quo, in which Asia continues to be powerless before Western economic superiority. Stability is, of course, necessary for healthy economic growth, but in a less developed country it can also mean stagnation. Sometimes the most dynamic and hopeful elements in an Asian country feel themselves forced into opposition to us because we seem to be the chief supporters of the status quo. Progress to them appears to demand anti-Americanism. In reaction to us and the status quo they think we support, they sometimes even join the Communists as the group that most insistently claims it will sweep away both America and the unhappy past. Thus our best potential allies in the effort to bring progress to Asia can turn into our most determined enemies.

This problem is not just one of appearances. Our aid must be channeled for the most part through existing political regimes, and thus it does help to bolster and maintain the political status quo and to slow down political change, good as well as bad. If the existing regime is not economically forward-moving or is inefficient or seriously corrupt, our aid, though designed to foster economic growth, can end up by inhibiting it. The danger that our aid will prove an adverse influence in Asia is heightened by the fact that those who are likely to seek our support most vigorously are exactly those who feel most threatened by popular discontent and the threat of change. Such governments may in time find themselves devoting most of their energies as well as our aid to the suppression of "subversion." Unfortunately, included in this "subversion" may be most of the drives for economic and social progress. Thus our sincere efforts to foster progress can end up by opposing it.

The United States has been accused of showing the arrogance of power. Actually I feel that, despite our great power, we have shown extraordinarily little arrogance, but we have often been too unconscious of the vast influence we exert and the sometimes adverse effect it has. We might more correctly be accused of showing naïveté in the use of power. Our well-intentioned aid or military presence can, without our realizing it, greatly alter the balance of forces within a country. All too often this influence can, in the name of stability, prop up an unsatisfactory status quo, and thus inhibit desirable change. We can find ourselves underwriting inefficiency or even backwardness. We run the risk of drifting unconsciously into a position of standing for the status quo rather than change in a part of the world that needs change desperately and undoubtedly will have it. When we do this, we condemn ourselves to what in the long run must be the losing side.

10. *The Balance of Power*

Perhaps our greatest mistake has been to assume that balance-of-power considerations were the same in Asia as in Europe. Soviet domination of a great industrialized nation like West Germany would obviously have produced an immediate and marked shift in the world balance of power. But it is hard to see how Soviet or Chinese domination over most of the countries of Asia could have any appreciable effect in the near future, except to weaken the dominating power.

The countries that have made significant progress toward economic modernization, such as Taiwan, South Korea, and Malaysia, might be of some value to the dominating power, but these are precisely the areas most resistant to Communist domination. Control over the rice-surplus areas, such as South Vietnam, Thailand, and Burma, might have certain economic advantages, but the costs of military conquest or political domination of these areas would far outweigh the economic benefits. Laos, as a deficit area, would be a serious economic drain as well as a military problem for any country that sought to control it. Domination of India would saddle the dominator with the huge Indian food problem, which would obviously be far beyond the capacities of either the Soviet Union or China to carry. The economic burdens resulting from any spread of Communism in Asia might more than offset the possible strategic gains. The domination of the whole of Asia by the Soviet Union, China, or both together could prove an unbearable load.

Of course, all this is completely unrealistic. As we have seen from our consideration of nationalism in Asia, external domination would be extremely difficult and costly to maintain even in small, selected areas in Asia, to say nothing of large nations like India or wide areas like Southeast Asia. Indirect domination through home-grown Communist movements would be more feasible, but such regimes would be certain to try to cast off foreign influence. The Communist world, already disrupted by the Sino-Soviet rift and the Yugoslav-Soviet estrangement, would not be strengthened by a Sino-Indian rift or a Sino-Burmese estrangement. On the other hand, the loss of Asian countries, either to Chinese or Soviet control or to domestic Communists, scarcely weakens us. It would only reduce our burdens, at least for the time being, allowing us and the other advanced non-Communist nations to concentrate our efforts more effectively elsewhere.

We also should not assume that the seizure of a nation in Asia, either by foreign-dominated or independent Communists, means that for all time that country is committed to Communism and to hostility toward us. Communism is no more resistant to change than are other systems. It, like other dictatorial systems, may be easier to operate in much of Asia than is democracy, and the socialist economy it espouses may have greater immediate appeal there than does a free economy. But Communist regimes are sure to disappoint Asian hopes as much as other systems do, and probably more. Efforts to remake human nature, as under the Maoists in China, are certain to fail. The attempt to control all economic activity in a less developed country with its low level of skills is likely to prove disastrous in agriculture and unduly restraining even in industrial development. Since Asian countries are as yet basically unstable and will undoubtedly go through many changes in the future, it seems probable that any of them that accepts Communism at this stage will in time evolve from its original Communist state or move entirely out of the Communist pattern again. In other words, a detour into Communism today will not necessarily have a decisive influence on what an Asian country is like some decades from now, when its attitudes and role in the world may be far more important to us than they are at present.

Much of the American fear of Communism in Asia seems to me to be based on an overestimation of its strengths. Those who most loudly trumpet hatred of Communism often appear to pay it the most respect. They credit Communists with being seven feet tall. They overlook their feet of clay. They seem to assume that Communists will achieve far greater economic growth than non-Communists, that they can permanently suppress the natural selfish desires of individuals and their yearnings for personal freedom, that they can counter the flood tides of nationalism, that they can either stop or control change in the complex development of great nations. They seem to assume that our more flexible, mixed economic system will not do as well, that the combination of personal freedom and affluence that our system offers does not have greater appeal than the regimentation and relative poverty of Communism, that our acceptance of diversity does not accommodate the tides of nationalism better than does Communism, and that our diversity and flexibility cannot deal more successfully with the problems of change. If these two sets of propositions were true, Communism would probably win out in any case, no matter what we tried to do, but fortunately they are not.

We should realize that our concepts of an international society made up of many independent and domestically differing units fits in with the forces of nationalism, while Communism does not. In other words, it is the Communists, not we, who in this respect are trying to stem the tides of history. We should see that our concepts of a free and affluent society are a far greater challenge to the status quo of Asia than are Communism's dictatorial rule and drab uniformity. In other words, we hold out far greater hopes to Asians.

We should have more confidence in both the appeal and the long-range effectiveness in Asia, as elsewhere in the world, of our concepts of a world order of diversity, a flexible mixed economy, social systems that permit individual freedom and dignity, and democratic political institutions that make possible such free systems. I do not expect that most Asian countries will come to mirror our institutions and our values. They will, no doubt, continue to maintain their own specific identities. Still, we should have more confidence in our ideals and institutions and in the good sense of Asians in coming to see their superiority over what Communism has to offer. In any case, however, our ideals can have influence in Asia only through their inherent appeal to people there and their effectiveness in practice. They cannot be imposed from without or defended by outsiders.

My own reading of recent Asian history makes me feel that neither a global Communist movement, nor Chinese neo-imperialism, nor a series of independent Communist movements is likely to establish a temporary hold, much less a permanent grip, over the greater part of what is now non-Communist Asia. But even assuming that any of these situations should materialize, I still feel that we Americans, of all people in the world, can face such a development with equanimity. It would be a tragedy for Asians; it might crush the hopes for the United Nations that small and weak nations embrace with particular intensity; it might threaten vital Japanese and Australian interests; the Soviet Union would almost certainly view Chinese domination of Asia with dismay; even Europeans might have reason for unease. But we in North America would have the least to worry about. The United States is so extremely rich and strong and so far away from Asia. We would not be threatened by the kind of military power Asia could develop, and we are not dependent in any way on Asia. As long as we continued to solve our own social and economic difficulties and to meet the problems of our relationship with the other advanced nations, particularly the Soviet Union, we would need have no fears for ourselves.

A Communization of much of Asia would merely further widen the gap between the advanced and the less developed nations and place a heavier burden on Communism in its competition with the free world. To be sure it would postpone our hopes for achieving world peace through greater worldwide prosperity and stability. The problems of North-South relations would be intensified and extended farther into the future. But we of all the nations of the world would probably suffer least from this.

We should therefore be the most relaxed of all nations in facing the problems of Asia and thus the best able to muster the patience, tolerance, and long-range foresight that are required. Asians, despite all the fabled patience of the East, cannot be expected to be patient in the face of their pressing problems, but we, despite our traditional impatience, can most easily take the long view. We should be able to direct our tremendous potential for aiding Asia into long-range constructive efforts and avoid having our strength dissipated in short-run, frustrating combat, as in Vietnam.

11. Re-evaluating the Problem

I have concentrated on our misunderstandings and errors in our relationship with Asia since the Second World War. I do not mean to condemn all that we have done. Many, perhaps most, of our actions have been basically sound. We have had great successes, along with our failures. What we achieved in Europe, in the occupation of Japan, and in the relations between the advanced nations contrasts sharply with the dismal aftermath of the First World War. In Asia, our response to aggression in Korea was daring and costly but basically correct. Even our efforts to give security to weak Asian states through SEATO and other alliances was well motivated and may have had some efficacy. Our great aid program to the less developed parts of the world has proved a major breakthrough in international relations. We have led the way in the concept that aid should be provided, not just to immediate allies of potential influence in world affairs, but to weak countries, whether or not they are aligned with us and however little their weight in the balance of power. Our aid efforts have constituted, not just a generous, but a statesmanlike approach to the great looming problem of the relationship between the rich and the poor sectors of the world.

We should be proud of the record of the past two and a half decades. As a people only just shaking ourselves awake from the long dream of isolation, we rose magnificently to the challenge of the Second World War and its aftermath, when we found ourselves the paramount power in the world and the only major nation not seriously disrupted by the long conflict. Unfamiliar though we were with this role of world leadership, we moved forward with boldness, imagination, and unparalleled generosity to meet our responsibilities. It is not surprising that, because of inexperience and ignorance, especially with regard to areas like Asia, we made a number of serious mistakes and used our strength less effectively than we might have. In Asia we may not deserve *A* for achievement, but we certainly deserve it for effort.

Times, however, have changed considerably in the twenty-two years since the end of the war. The other advanced nations are all now fully restored and stronger than ever. The once colonial and semicolonial areas are constituted into independent and nationalistically self-assertive countries. The world leans much less heavily on our strength and leadership.

Also, we have learned a great deal in the meantime. We have had a wealth of experience in our leadership role. We have come to know much more about all parts of the world. We have seen our earlier assumptions about the problems we faced in Asia confirmed, modified, or invalidated by the test of history. We need no longer base our policies toward this area on hasty analogies drawn from other times and other places. We are now able to develop a far clearer concept of what Asia means to us than we could in the confused early postwar years or under the psychological stresses of the cold war. We also can see more clearly what the long-range goals should be, what the possibilities are, where our limitations lie, and how we can best use our tremendous assets in helping Asia toward a happier future for Asians and for us. We can see that what is needed is a long-range, constructive approach to Asia's problems, not a short-range, defensive one.

The Vietnam War makes this rethinking of our policies all the more imperative. It has helped educate us, painfully but convincingly, about our problems in Asia. It has clearly shown the danger that our strength, if used unwisely in Asia, can be dissipated in fruitless friction or can even produce strong countercurrents. We see all too clearly how limited our military power is in guerrilla warfare, how our military presence tends to make our opponents seem to be the true nationalists, how military destruction and disruption nullify our efforts at economic and social development, and how our involvement in war in one small area can have adverse repercussions far afield.

Even more important, we face the imminent danger that the frustrations of the Vietnam War may lead us into still more unsound policies in Asia, unless we start right now to think through our problems more carefully than we have to date. If we do not do this, we may make the mistake of trying to recoup past blunders by increasing our military efforts to force Asians to conform to our wishes. An even more likely danger is that we may turn our backs on Asia's problems and withdraw across the international railroad tracks to the pleasant suburbs of Northern prosperity. This above all times is the moment in history when we must re-think, carefully and fundamentally, our whole relationship with Asia.

Chapter Three

Toward
a
New
Asian
Policy

IT IS sometimes easier to outline general principles than to apply these principles to specific cases. A compass can show the direction in which we wish to go, but the actual route will be determined by the immediate lay of the land. If we do not have our general bearings, no route is likely to lead us to our goal, but even when we have our bearings, we still may be forced to follow a somewhat tortuous course.

We should also bear in mind that the United States is a huge ship of state. Its steering mechanism is an extremely complicated process that would defy a Rube Goldberg to portray. It changes course only slowly and ponderously, and, when it does, it affects the courses of all the other ships of state on the shrinking seas of international relations. The Soviet Union is the only other one which is at all of comparable size. The rest are far smaller, some mere cockleshells. United States policy creates much of the world environment for these other nations. Our smallest move can have great significance for them. We must therefore be very careful and also clear in any change of course we make. We cannot suddenly shift to an entirely new course but can only make careful moves in that direction as opportunity offers. Thus we can only move slowly and cautiously toward a new Asian policy.

We must also remember that general principles cannot be applied simply and uniformly across the board, particularly in an area as large and diversified as Asia. In this book, I have fallen into one of our commonest semantic errors—to speak of Asia as if it were a single unit. "Asia," even in the restricted sense in which I have used it, is simply a "cover word" for half the whole world. This region embraces two of the world's great zones of differing civilizations —the Chinese in East Asia and the Indian in South Asia. While economically these two civilization types may resemble each other today—they are both poor—in more fundamental ways, such as in underlying philosophy, social organization, and political concepts, they have throughout history constituted the two extremes of human development. The Chinese type has tended toward this-worldly, pragmatic activism, social homogeneity, and a central focus on the political unit; the Indian type, at least at its higher levels, has tended toward other-worldly, spiritual passivity, social fragmentation, and a religious rather than political orientation of society. Our own ancient Mediterranean zone of civilization, which later bifurcated into the Western and Islamic types of culture, stands in these respects in between the Indian and Chinese extremes.

Within these major zones of civilization, too, there is great geographic and cultural diversity. Each of the many countries of Asia is itself a unique case, and several contain a series of distinct entities. While general principles are necessary if we are to maintain our bearings amid this welter of diversity, American policy toward the many countries of Asia cannot be a uniform machine-made product, but must be specially tailored to each situation.

I cannot, of course, in the brief compass of this small volume delve deeply into the unique circumstances of each country and determine how our general principles might best apply to the situation there, but, if we are to come to grips with what we face in Asia, we must consider some of the specific areas and problems and outline some of the concrete steps we should take.

I

Japan

❦

IN MY definition of Asia in the preceding chapter, I excluded Japan, but in our more detailed consideration of our relations with Asia, we must start with this country. As the only great modernized nation in that part of the world, it is coming to be an important factor in the whole region. What it is, the role it chooses to play in Asia, and the relations it has with us will increasingly influence the nature of our own relationship with the rest of Asia.

1. *Japan Today*

In recent years Japan has sunk from fifth to seventh place in population among the nations of the world, having been passed by both Indonesia and Pakistan. At the same time, however, it has been rising rapidly in economic productivity. It has passed Italy and China and is now in the process of passing the United Kingdom and France, to become the fourth nation in the world in GNP, behind only ourselves, the Soviet Union, and West Germany. Today Japan is one of the industrial giants of the world. It produces more ships than the next three nations combined and stands first in production of television sets and radios, second in production of automobiles and trucks, third in steel, and fourth in electric power.

For many years the economy of Japan has been growing faster than that of any other major country in the world. It has averaged close to 10 per cent per year after one has discounted the effects of inflation. While the rest of the world is trying to accelerate growth, the Japanese government is attempting to keep real growth down to around 8 per cent per year, in order to reduce the severe social dislocations that inevitably accompany an overly high rate of economic expansion. It failed to keep the lid fully on in 1966, growing 9.7 per cent in real terms. Meanwhile, population has been rising at a rate of 1 per cent per year or less, leaving net increases of around 7 to 9 per cent in per capita wealth. Fifteen years ago, Japanese individual monetary incomes tended to be about one tenth those for Americans in corresponding positions, but today they have risen to about one fourth of ours and have drawn abreast or passed those of South Europe.

Japan's economic surge is even more startling when measured against the rest of Asia and the other less developed areas. As we have seen, the 100 million people of Japan produce more wealth than the 700 million Chinese. If we mentally subtract minimum "subsistence rations" for 100 million people from Japan's GNP and 700 million such rations from China's GNP, we will see that the Japanese have vastly more wealth left over with which to do something beyond surviving. The Japanese GNP equals that of all Latin America put together, is double that for the whole of Africa, is twice that of India, which has a population of 475 million, and exceeds that of all the rest of geographic Asia, from Turkey, Israel, and the Arab states through Korea and Taiwan, once India and China have been subtracted from the total. Japanese per capita income averages about 8 times that of the other countries of Asia.

Japan's economic achievements are paralleled by comparable developments in education and in social, legal, and political institutions. Without these, this great economic progress would not have been possible. For some generations now, literacy in Japan has been almost as close to 100 per cent as is possible in any society. With more than 20 per cent of college-age people in institutions of higher learning, it ranks perhaps third in the world in this category and well above any European country. It has a very stable, entirely orderly, middle-class type of society. Despite its spotty political record before the Second World War and the great disruption of its defeat, Japan since 1945 has maintained a remarkably steady political course through parliamentary democracy. Guerrilla insurgencies or even *coups d'état* seem no more possible there than in the advanced democracies of the West.

Our connections with Japan have become huge, intricate, and mutually rewarding. Our trade with it has passed the five-billion-dollar mark, ranking second only to our trade with Canada and far ahead of our trade with any European country. This is the largest trade that has ever flowed between two countries separated by an ocean. It accounts for close to 30 per cent of Japan's total foreign commerce and around 9 per cent of our own. Japan is our biggest commercial (as opposed to giveaway) market for our agricultural surpluses. It has overwhelmingly more cultural and intellectual contacts with us than with any other nation in the world. For us these cultural and intellectual contacts are comparable to those with our major allies in Europe and far more important than those with any other part of the non-Western world.

2. *The Lessons of Japan's Modernization*

Japan's position today and its relationship with the United States are happy harbingers of what the world might someday be. When threatened in the nineteenth century by Western military and economic superiority, Japan reacted forcefully and, in its mad scramble to catch up with the West, proved to be a serious disturber of world peace. But now that it has caught up, it has become a force for stability in a troubled world and an enricher of all those who have contact with it. The vastly beneficial relations, both economic and cultural, that Japan and the United States have established with each other show what can develop throughout the world when the other non-Western nations have come closer abreast with the countries of the West.

Japan's century of modernization provides other insights into the promises and also the dangers of the modernization process elsewhere in Asia. We have seen that Japan's early success in industrialization was based on foundations of a type that have not been fully laid in much of Asia. This suggests that the preparatory stages for economic modernization may be slow and difficult.

Japan's recent history also shows that the early stages in modernization can create difficult new problems, while solving old ones. It suggests that, as the modernization process gains momentum, the countries of Asia, even if they develop more internal stability, may become more upsetting to the peace and stability of the world around them. In the case of Japan, as it gained in power, it changed from a menaced nation to a menacer. As it moved away from its traditional moorings, it became a spiritually more disturbed country. Ideas and attitudes did not keep pace with changes in the economy and society. The firm unity of the early modernizers was not passed on to the next generation of leaders and broke down still more in the third generation. Japan in the 1920's entered into a political "time of troubles," from which it is only just emerging today.

As Japan modernized, its new technology and high educational standards made it possible for it to be either a working democracy or a fully totalitarian state. Nations that have gone through little of the modernization process cannot really be either, because they lack the high level of skills that both systems require. They are likely to be inefficient dictatorships, or incomplete, limping democracies, or a combination of the two. Even partially modernized nations, like Russia after its revolution or China today, while able to operate totalitarian systems, may not be capable of conducting their affairs through the more complicated techniques of democracy.

Thoroughly modernized nations, however, face the choice between a full totalitarianism and full democracy. The citizens have so high a degree of education that, unless they are heavily indoctrinated and carefully controlled in the totalitarian manner, they will demand meaningful participation in government decisions through democracy. They are no longer the uneducated, inert masses of pre-industrial societies. The Japanese, unsure of what new values modernization had brought them, wavered between democracy and totalitarianism, as did other late starters in the modernization process, such as Germany and Italy. Out of the indecision and travail of these countries came Fascism, Naziism, and Japan's militaristic adventurism, which so disturbed the world for two decades.

We must hope that the other countries of Asia will profit from Japan's mistakes. We should not, however, be surprised if many Asian countries become more fundamentally troubled within themselves and more troublesome to their neighbors as modernization progresses. This is an additional reason for expecting instability to continue in Asia for a long time.

Modern Japan teaches a more hopeful lesson about the survival of non-Western cultures. In the early days of Japan's modernization, it seemed that the native culture was being swept away by a tidal wave of Westernization. Japan, some people felt, would become a rootless Asian outpost of Western civilization. As we look at the situation today, however, we see how strong Japanese cultural traits remain. Japan is without doubt the most culturally distinctive of the modernized nations. It is exceedingly Japanese.

True, Japan has all the technology and gadgetry of the modern world, but we must distinguish between modernization and Westernization. What makes railroad trains or television Western and not Japanese? We had only a three- or four-decade jump over the Japanese in railways, and now they far outperform us in this field. In television our head start was only a few years, and now the whole electronics field is as much theirs as ours. On the other hand, Japan is the only country in the world that builds true mammoth tankers, but that does not make such vessels culturally Japanese rather than Occidental. The contrast between modernization and Westernization might best be seen by comparing the statistics in Japan for television sets, which are something purely modern, and Christianity, a major element in traditional Western culture. Some 93 per cent of Japanese homes have televisions sets, but only about 0.5 per cent of the Japanese are professing Christians.

We sometimes forget how much we ourselves have changed through technological and institutional modernization. An American resurrected from the year 1700 would be almost as baffled by contemporary New York as a Japanese of 1700 would be by modern Tokyo. To both, railroads, airplanes, and television would, of course, be entirely unfamiliar, but so also would compulsory universal education, labor unions, professional baseball, Rotary Clubs, and the P-TA—to say nothing of the whole nature and pace of modern life. In some ways our Japanese of 1700 might feel more at home with modern design and modern art than would his American contemporary.

Modernization and Westernization, of course, are inevitably mixed up with each other even in Japan. Modern technology and the modern institutions and social trends that have gone along with it appeared first in the West, where they often became deeply imbued with Western cultural traits. From music and religion to haircuts and neckties, these accompanied modern technology and institutions into Japan. They have modified and enriched Japanese culture. Christian ideas are far more influential in Japan than the low number of converts would suggest. Baseball is Japan's national sport. Tokyo supports five full-scale and fully professional symphony orchestras, a claim I doubt that any other city in the world can make.

At the same time much of Japan's traditional culture remains vibrantly alive. In fact, most of the higher forms of Japanese culture seem to have a great deal more vitality today than they did during the earlier onslaught of Western influence. Basic Japanese aesthetic concepts—such as the feeling for color, space, and asymmetry—have survived into contemporary times far better than many of our own traditional aesthetic values. Japanese cultural influences—from karate and judo to woodblock prints and pottery, from landscape gardening and interior decorating to poetry and drama, from Zen to flower arrangement—are flowing out of a now thoroughly modernized Japan and are having a cultural impact on the Western world of a sort no non-Western culture has ever had before. While the Japanese have been enriched by importing much of our traditional culture, we are now being enriched by importing much of theirs.

Japan's cultural survival as a distinct entity and its ability to assimilate much of the cultural tradition of the West while holding on to its own are happy auguries for the future. We can take hope that some, perhaps most, of the other non-Western cultures will survive the modernization-Westernization wave. If they do, we all shall be culturally the richer for it.

3. *Japan's Role in the World*

Because of Japan's great economic power and its tremendous lead over the rest of Asia, one would assume that it would be playing a major role in world affairs. But it is not. In fact, for most of the twenty-two years since the end of the war, it has been a virtual cipher in international affairs.

There are good reasons for this seemingly anomalous situation. During much of the postwar period, Japan was not what she is today. At the end of the war, she was probably the most thoroughly destroyed of the major participants and certainly the most demoralized. The Japanese had been cut off by our submarines from the sources of raw materials on which they lived; their highly inflammable cities had been virtually wiped out by our bombers; and the people, victims of the intensive indoctrination of their military masters, were thoroughly disillusioned and bewildered by the collapse of the country. Recovery of the economy came more slowly than in any of the other major war-torn lands, and national morale lagged even further behind. In any case, Japan was no longer an independent nation. For almost seven years, it remained under the firm control of the American military occupation.

Even when the Japanese recovered their independence through the Peace Treaty in March 1952, they showed no desire to play a role in the outside world. The economy was only beginning to move forward again, and there still remained serious doubts that Japan, because of its very narrow and poor geographic base, could develop a truly viable economy over the long run. The people also were deeply divided politically on almost every issue. Various Marxist-oriented parties of the opposition stood in firm confrontation with the conservative majority that controlled the government. The political future was unclear and seemed fraught with dangers.

The Japanese also had lost confidence in themselves. They had brought catastrophe on themselves and destruction on their neighbors through their militaristic course. They felt that they had nothing of value to offer others but must look abroad—to the United States or possibly to the Soviet Union or Communist China—for guidance. Japan in actuality was still almost entirely dependent on the United States for defense, as provided for in the Security Treaty negotiated just before the Peace Treaty went into effect. It also remained somewhat dependent on American economic aid and still more on the American market for close to a third of its exports. It thus seemed doomed to subservience to the United States.

Most countries welcomed Japan's international passivity. Japan was remembered with fear and hatred as the disturber of the peace in the Far East. Its neighbors were happy to see it impotent, and their hostility and suspicion were added reasons for the Japanese to eschew any active role abroad. Thus Japan's own problems remained so overwhelming and its freedom of action abroad so circumscribed that the Japanese felt they must limit themselves to working on their own domestic problems and should leave international affairs to the United States and other healthier countries.

These conditions changed only slowly, but by the mid-1960's Japan was obviously entering a new phase of its history. Economic progress had by this time become so spectacular that the Japanese could not help but take pride in themselves. Their self-confidence was slowly returning. However heinous Japanese errors had been, their overall record during the past century had been one of unequaled success in Asia. Japan was obviously a strong country and had something to offer the world. Moreover, the continuing instabilities and slow economic progress of the rest of Asia made the Japanese apprehensive about the environment in which they lived. It became evident that if the Japanese wished a better, safer and more prosperous world in which to live, they too would have to contribute to its development.

Meanwhile the resentments of Japan's neighbors had also abated. The Koreans, who had suffered from forty years of cruel Japanese colonialism, feared and hated Japan the most, though they also had a deep sense of respect and admiration. The Filipinos, whose island had been twice despoiled by the Japanese during the Second World War, remained bitter. Some strong animosities survived in Singapore and Malaysia. But otherwise anti-Japanese sentiments had largely subsided. Other fears and hatreds had interposed themselves, and Japan was remembered as much with gratitude for the destruction of colonialism as with condemnation for the cruelties of the war. Even the Koreans and Filipinos were ready to welcome the Japanese back onto the international scene as a possible source of aid to them.

During the past two or three years Japan has been cautiously venturing out again into international politics. The Japanese are in search of a role for themselves in the world. Their past failures, their domestic political divisions, and the remaining animosities of their neighbors will make them move slowly. Over the next five to ten years, however, Japan is likely to come out fully into the world to play a role somewhat more commensurate with its great size.

This role is not likely to be military. The Japanese, in reaction to the disastrous wars into which their military masters led them, have become the most thoroughly pacifistic people in the world. In their new Constitution of 1947, they stated that they "forever renounce war as a sovereign right of the nation," and they promised that "land, sea and air forces, as well as other war potential, will never be maintained." In time they came to interpret the Constitution as permitting self-defense, and today they have land, sea, and air "Self Defense Forces" totaling around 240,000 men. The great bulk of the people, however, while supporting the Self Defense Forces, remain adamantly set against any military role overseas. Their revulsion for war and militarism is very strong and will not quickly change.

It is sometimes argued that Japan, as a sort of military eunuch, must continue to be a cipher in international affairs. I personally would not agree. The world already has such a military balance of terror between the two great powers that the military strength of other countries has relatively little bearing on the world balance of power and becomes a matter of only localized significance. It is hard to see what advantage it would be to Japan to greatly increase its military power—as long as the United States continues to maintain a stabilizing military presence in the Western Pacific. Japan does not need to duplicate our Seventh Fleet, nor would there be much point in its holding a second nuclear umbrella under our larger one. As an island nation, its defense problems are relatively simple. Moreover, in Asia even the vast military power we have is not very effective against the major threat to the less developed countries, which is internal instability.

On the other hand, a remilitarized Japan would frighten its neighbors and thus perhaps reduce its influence rather than increase it. The costs of remilitarization would also cut into Japanese prosperity and diminish the economic aid Japan might otherwise be able to offer. Because of their very light military burdens, the Japanese should have no difficulty in reaching the figure of 1 per cent of GNP for aid purposes, set as a target by the advanced nations. In fact, they might be able to exceed it, converting the 3 or 4 per cent more of GNP that other advanced countries of similar size put into defense into an extra 1 per cent for foreign aid. Since economic growth is far more important for the future of Asia than defense against aggression, an attempt to play a larger military role would probably reduce Japan's long-range contribution, not only to the economic progress of Asia, but also to its stability.

Japan's chief role will probably be as a supplier of economic aid and technological know-how. It is already a major trading partner for South Korea, Taiwan, and the countries of Southeast Asia, and through reparations programs it has supplied considerable amounts of what might be called involuntary aid. As Japan starts to phase out of reparations, it is shifting increasingly to voluntary aid, in the form of commercial credits and, increasingly, as "soft" loans and even outright grants. In 1965 it finally normalized its relations with South Korea, promising $300 million in grants, $200 million in soft loans, and more millions in commercial credits. After the anti-Communist coup in Indonesia, it took the lead among the creditor countries in working out better terms of credit for the new regime. When the Asian Development Bank was set up in 1966 as a major new source of development funds for Asia, Japan provided a sum equal to our $200 million contribution, thus becoming the first country since the war to match us in any major enterprise of this sort. Japan has already become, next to the United States, the chief source of economic aid for this part of the world, and its role will almost certainly continue to grow.

Japan has also become an important source of technological skills for East and South Asia. Actually its experience in industrialization and institutional modernization may be more relevant for this part of the world than is our own, or that of Western Europe or the Soviet Union. Japan's experience has been achieved under geographic and cultural conditions—a rice agriculture, heavy population densities, and a non-Western cultural background—more like those of the rest of Asia than has the experience in modernization of the countries of the West. This is particularly true of the United States and the Soviet Union, which have a much more favorable balance between people and natural resources than does most of Asia.

The Japanese for some years have been bringing hundreds of South Asian students to Japan for advanced training, largely in the technical fields. They have launched a small program similar to the Peace Corps and have sent some members of it as far afield as Africa. They face a major language barrier, however, in their efforts to transmit technological skills to others. Japanese is a difficult language, very different from those of other Asian countries, except Korea, and its writing system is perhaps the most complicated in the world. Other Asians, who often are competent in English or one of the other international languages, find Japanese hard to learn and less rewarding in the long run than languages that have wider international currency. The Japanese on their side are notably poor linguists. If they are to play as large a role in technological aid as they should, they may have to develop technological institutions in Japan where the language of instruction is English. Even more important would be to modernize their own methods of English instruction, so that the tremendous efforts young Japanese put into learning English would produce better results. This might also increase Japanese efficiency in international trade and would greatly magnify Japan's now somewhat inarticulate voice in world affairs.

Japan may also have an important role of inspiration, even of leadership, in Asia. As it emerges from its postwar isolationism, and Asian nations become, as a result, increasingly aware of Japan, its example as a non-Western country that has achieved affluence through a free and democratic society will have a growing influence throughout Asia. As we have seen, affluence and personal freedom have more attractiveness for Asians, too, than does Communist China's drab uniformity and regimentation. Japan has shown that affluence and personal freedom are not necessarily limited to the Occidental sector of mankind but can be achieved by others too. As we have seen, Japan's defeat of Russia in 1904–5 was the original inspiration for the nationalist movements that finally swept Asia after the Second World War. Perhaps in the next few years the Japanese example will again prove a source of even more constructive inspiration to the rest of Asia.

Leadership in Asia would be harder to provide. No Asian countries are looking to others for leadership, and, in any case, the Japanese, in their continuing mood of caution and self-doubt, are not likely to wish to provide it. The phrase "we Asians" comes quickly to Asian lips, but in actuality Asian peoples know relatively little about one another and harbor strong mutual prejudices. Unless the Japanese try harder than they have to develop better skills at communication and a more sensitive understanding of their neighbors, we may in time hear as much about the "ugly Japanese" as we have about the "ugly American." No country, I believe, is likely to become "the leader" of Asia.

Still, it is extremely significant that in geographic Asia there is one large nation that is strong economically and is thoroughly modernized. Japan's presence in regional groupings gives these groupings a great deal more meaning and solidity than if all the members were weak and less developed. As Asian racially and in cultural background, Japan can perhaps play a bigger and more useful role in the healthy development of East and South Asia than can any other modernized country, even including such giants as ourselves and the Soviet Union. In fact, as the one major country that straddles the greatest rift in the world, being an industrialized nation of the "North" on the one side but a non-Western, non-Caucasian nation on the other, Japan may have a uniquely useful role in world history over the next several decades.

What Japan has become today and the role it gives promise of playing in the future are, I believe, two good reasons for us to be basically optimistic about the future of Asia. Japan was the major disturber of the Far East before the war and since its end has figured little one way or the other, but now it is emerging as a strong new force for stability and healthy progress. What it does will probably be more important for the future of Asia than anything China does, at least in the next generation or two. While the outcome of the Vietnam War is a matter of keen immediate interest, particularly to Americans, the role Japan decides to play will in the long run be far more important for Asians and for Americans, too, than the outcome in Vietnam.

From all this one can see quite clearly that Japan's future and our relationship with it are of much greater long-range importance to us than anything else in the vast area on the other side of the Pacific. The economic and other benefits to us of our present relationship with Japan probably outweigh the benefits of our relationship with all the rest of Asia put together. In the foreseeable future, we have much more to hope for from Japan than from the rest of Asia combined. If Japan were to falter economically or politically or if it were to become hostile to us, our hopes for the rest of Asia too would probably fade.

Our interest in the future of Japan and in our relations with it are comparable to our interest in Western Europe, even if on a smaller scale. The countries of Western Europe, taken collectively, are much larger than Japan and figure more directly in the balance of power with the Soviet Union. At the same time, the very fact that Japan stands alone as the only major modernized nation in a huge area of instability and backwardness makes it more important to us than are countries of comparable economic size in Europe.

4. Political Trends

Despite the many serious problems facing Japan, I believe there is good reason for optimism with regard both to its continuing prosperity and stability and to its continuing friendship with us. It is true that Japan balances somewhat precariously on a narrow geographic base and thus is very dependent on world trade. As we shall see, it is politically a deeply divided nation. In its frantic pace of economic growth, it has seriously slighted the public sector of the economy in the postwar era. Housing is most inadequate. The problems of urban crowding and pollution are particularly severe because of the huge numbers of people crammed into the narrow coastal plains of Japan. Urbanization, modernization, and affluence have brought the Japanese many of the social ills we have experienced recently. They have some juvenile delinquency, though not so much as we. The greater speed of change in Japan has made the gap in understanding and communication between generations even more severe than in the United States. There is also a strong feeling among Japanese that their democratic institutions are undermined by corruption and voter apathy. They feel a sense of a spiritual vacuum—a lack of a new national "value system" to replace that of the authoritarian and militaristic past.

These are all grave problems, but Japan is facing them honestly and with about the same degree of success as other advanced nations. In spite of the spiritual confusion and the vehemence of political debate, the Japanese are far more united on basic matters than they seem to realize. There is overwhelming support for a peaceful role for Japan in the world and for a just international order under the United Nations. There is equally strong support for the new Constitution and for its clear-cut parliamentary democracy and broad individual rights. Only a small fringe on the extreme left and an even smaller fringe on the extreme right can envision anything but a democratic form of government for Japan.

There are actually few places in the world where the economic and political prognosis looks more favorable. Japan lacks the deep democratic roots of the English-speaking countries and some North European lands, but after these, its democracy is as firmly founded as anywhere in the world, being at least as stable as that of Germany, France, or Italy. The only great threat to Japan would be a world holocaust or a major worldwide depression, but, if either of these occurred, we ourselves would have many other problems to worry about more serious than Japan's future.

Japan's continued friendship with us may be a matter of greater doubt. To understand this problem we might briefly review the recent history of domestic politics in Japan. The Japanese emerged from the Second World War a confused and deeply divided people. A conservative majority, however, has been in control of the government ever since 1948. It centers around the Liberal Democratic Party, the heir of the two major prewar parliamentary parties. The Liberal Democrats draw their chief voting strength from rural and small-town Japan and their prestige and power from their close association with big business and the bureaucracy.

In opposition stand the Marxist parties of the left. As the most daring and vocal opponents of the disastrous prewar course of the militarists, the Marxists emerged from Japan's defeat as seemingly the most obvious alternative to militarism. Throughout they have proclaimed themselves the champions of peace and are commonly called the "progressives." They draw their strength largely from organized labor and from the intellectual and white-collar residents of the cities, whom the Japanese call by a very appropriate English term they have coined—"salary man."

In theory, the leftist parties are for a socialized economy, but, because of Japan's great economic success, their demands are somewhat muted on that side. A much more central issue of political debate is the problem of Japan's defense alignment with the United States. According to the Marxists, "American imperialism," which they view as an inevitable product of our "capitalistic" society, is as great a problem to Japan and possibly a more pressing one than is its own "monopoly capitalism." They feel that the United States, driven by its "imperialistic" urges, is certain to clash with the Socialist "peace camp," meaning the Soviet Union and China. Hence the Security Treaty with the United States and the American bases in Japan, far from giving Japan security, actually threaten to embroil it in war. A neutralist Japan, even if virtually unarmed, would be safer, they feel, than one tied to the American war machine.

During the past two decades, Japanese politics have centered around this debate between neutralism and alignment with the United States. The huge demonstrations against the Security Treaty with the United States that swept Tokyo in the spring of 1960 were an outgrowth of it, though certain peripheral issues, such as constitutional procedures in parliament and fears that President Eisenhower's proposed visit would constitute foreign pressure on domestic policies, added fuel to the flames. The treaty as revised in 1960 put limitations on the use and the armament of our bases in Japan as well as a ten-year time limit, after which it could be repudiated by either side. We agreed neither to make major changes in armament in Japan (that is, to bring in nuclear weapons) nor to use the bases in direct military action elsewhere without "prior consultation" (meaning agreement) with the Japanese government. Thus the revised treaty was much more advantageous to the Japanese than the original treaty. The left, however, opposed it because the earlier treaty had been imposed on an occupied Japan, while the now independent Japanese government was fully responsible for the terms of the new treaty. The government won out in 1960, despite the massive popular protests. Ever since, opposition has aimed at 1970 as the year when the treaty can be denounced and the defense tie with the United States ended.

During the past twenty years the once large majority of the conservative government party has slowly dwindled. On the average, the voters seem to be shifting from it to the opposition parties at the rate of about 1 or 2 per cent per year. This seems basically a sociological rather than a political change. It reflects the rapid urbanization of Japan, the decline of rural populations, the growth of the "salary man" sector of society, and the shift of workers from small-scale, family enterprises to large-scale industries. In the general election of January 1967, the opposition parties together polled a total of 46 per cent of the vote, the remainder going to the Liberal Democrats and a handful of independents, most of whom were also conservative. At this rate, the opposition vote may exceed the 50-per-cent mark by or before 1970.

These voting trends are interpreted by some as foretelling a sharp break in our relationship with Japan in the near future, but this is too hasty a judgment. It overlooks the fact that the opposition is itself seriously divided. On the one hand, two of the opposition parties are more centrist than leftist. The Democratic Socialist Party, which won 7.5 per cent of the votes in the last general election, is essentially a post-Marxian movement, much like the socialist parties of Europe, and is strongly committed to parliamentary democracy and opposed to Communism. The Kōmeitō, the political wing of the Sōka Gakkai religious movement, which won 5.5 per cent of the vote, has no clearly defined political position but probably leans more toward the conservative side than to the left. The real left itself is also divided into two parties—the Communists, who won 5 per cent of the vote, and the Socialists, who won 28 per cent but are themselves deeply divided between a left wing that is at present more friendly to Peking than are even the Communists and a right wing that tends toward the Democratic Socialist position. Thus the opposition is divided four ways, and it seems highly improbable that it could ever coalesce into less than two groups—one pro-Communist and the other anti-Communist.

Another factor is that, while the vote has been drifting leftward, public opinion in Japan has been drifting toward the center. The labor unions, which underlie both the Socialist and Democratic Socialist Parties, have definitely moved toward moderation—that is, away from political agitation over global issues and toward concentration on the immediate interests of workers. The centrist parties and even the more moderate supporters of the Socialists have also gravitated slowly toward a more tolerant stand on the defense alliance with the United States and thus closer to a consensus with the conservatives. Even if the conservatives should lose their parliamentary majority in future elections, the most likely outcome seems to me not a government led by the left but a coalition between the conservatives and the more moderate elements of the opposition or possibly a coalescence of these elements with the more moderate wing of the right into a new centrist party. Thus a sharp break in Japan's relations with the United States does not seem probable.

5. *Problems in Our Relations with Japan*

The debate in Japan over the pros and cons of the Security Treaty is not the only strain on relations between Japan and the United States. The presence of some 40,000 American servicemen in our bases in Japan inevitably gives rise to a large number of local frictions. So also do the sound nuisance of our jet planes in a crowded country, the extension of runways in a land-hungry society, and the occasional crashes of our planes on Japanese homes.

More serious is our continued military occupation of the Ryukyu Islands, which before the war constituted the Japanese prefecture of Okinawa, named after the main island in the Ryukyus. Our extensive system of bases on Okinawa, unencumbered by the limitations placed on our bases in Japan, has become a major backup for our whole military posture in that part of the world. At the same time, however, foreign military rule over the 950,000 Okinawan Japanese more than two decades after the end of the war is a growing cause for irritation and concern even among conservative Japanese and is a dangerous focus for leftist opposition to the American alliance as the target date of 1970 approaches. We have recognized that "residual sovereignty" over Okinawa remains with Japan, meaning that the islands will "revert" to Japan when conditions in the Far East permit, but this promise is too vague to satisfy the immediate nationalistic feelings of Okinawans and Japanese.

Economic frictions have also loomed large in Japanese-American relations over the past fifteen years. There have been perennial disputes over salmon fisheries in the North Pacific, and the Japanese, depending as heavily as they do on the American market, are also extremely sensitive to any American resistance to Japanese imports. Despite our championing of freer worldwide trade, we have forced on the Japanese so-called "voluntary restrictions" that limit the volume of their exports to us in a wide range of items from textiles to baseball gloves. On the other side of the coin, American businessmen are very dissatisfied with the severe restraints that the Japanese government has maintained in one guise or another on American imports and also on the introduction of foreign capital into Japan. Not long ago the Japanese were so much aware of their economic dependence on our market that they liked to say that, when New York sneezed, Tokyo came down with pneumonia. In the past few years, as Japan has become economically stronger and more self-confident, these tensions have relaxed noticeably, but there still remains a handful of troublesome trade problems that serve as irritants in the huge and complex economic relationship between the two countries.

Our foreign policy toward Asia has also become an area of serious friction. While the Japanese government has always stayed close to American policy on China in the United Nations and gives full recognition to the Republic of China on Taiwan, the general public is extremely restive about

Japan's relations with China. The Japanese feel that because of their geographic propinquity, their special cultural relations with China throughout history, and their need to trade with everyone, including their great Chinese neighbor, Japan has much greater reason to desire full and friendly relations with Peking than does the United States. At the same time, they feel that, because of Japan's close alignment with the United States, American obstinacy has stood in the way of better relations between Tokyo and Peking. They regard this as the steep price they pay for their relationship with us.

In actuality, however, Japan does have important relations with Communist China. It is, in fact, China's biggest trading partner, and there is probably a bigger flow of people, for cultural or trading purposes, between China and Japan than between China and any other country. Tokyo does not recognize Peking, but this is basically because it recognizes Chiang's government on Taiwan, with which it has close relations and a very large trade. Japan could not do what France did in forcing a break of relations with Taiwan in order to recognize Peking, because Japan has far more important relations with Taiwan, as well as with Communist China, than does France.

The native Taiwanese show very warm feelings toward their former colonial masters, which pleases the Japanese, and they return these feelings. They also are grateful to Chiang Kai-shek for his quick repatriation of the Japanese soldiers and civilians stranded in China at the end of the war, in contrast to the Soviet Union's long imprisonment and harsh treatment of the Japanese it captured. Some Japanese also look on a Taiwan free of Peking's control as in Japanese interests. Thus Japanese involvement in Taiwan makes their China problem somewhat analogous to our own. In any case, America has not really stood between Japan and Communist China, and the incompleteness of the relationship between the two is basically because of Peking's intransigence and Japan's interest in Taiwan. Still, among the general public, Japan's unsatisfactory relationship with Communist China is blamed principally on the United States and serves as a major strain in the relations between the two countries.

As we have seen, the Vietnam War has become another important point of stress. When it was escalated by our bombing of the North in February 1965 and our subsequent injection of large land armies into the South, the Japanese public responded explosively in fear and dismay. They thought that Washington had become dominated by unthinking militarists, as had Tokyo in the 1930's, and that we would inevitably go on to war with Communist China and that Japan would then become involved because of our bases there and in Okinawa. They felt that we had embarked on a hopeless war with Asian nationalism, as they had during the 1930's and 1940's in China. As a nation all but wiped out by our bombing two decades earlier, they also identified themselves with the Vietnamese who were being bombed rather than with us. There were probably also racial sympathies in this identification. The government throughout has expressed its "understanding" of the American position but, in view of the strength of public feeling, has said no more. Since the latter part of 1965, feelings about Vietnam have subsided somewhat or at least leveled off, for the dire predictions of war with China have not materialized, but, as I have noted earlier, a further major escalation of the war in Vietnam could possibly destroy the whole Japanese-American relationship.

An important strain of a more general nature is the discrepancy in size between the two countries. We face this problem everywhere in the world, even with our major European allies and our closest neighbor, Canada. We are more than eight times Japan's size in economic power, and this already great discrepancy has been magnified by history. We represent the alien culture that destroyed Japan's "happy" isolation a century ago and threatened it with economic, if not political, subjugation. In the recent war we defeated and virtually destroyed Japan and then proceeded to occupy it and dictate its policies for seven years. Since then we have been its overpowering "big brother," defending it, providing it with its biggest market and most important economic contacts, and dominating its cultural relations with the outside world. It is easy for us to wish to deal on a basis of absolute equality with the Japanese, but it is hard for them to feel fully equal to us. The ills of the world—even of Japan itself —can all too easily be blamed on us. There is likely to be a big chip on the Japanese shoulder against the United States, or, if not that, at least a certain wariness and distrust.

All this contributes to a broad streak of anti-Americanism in Japan, but this we find in one form or another all over the world. It is the price we pay for our size and importance. In Japan it has special cultural and historical overtones. Much of the left is by definition anti-American. Among older conservatives are found the people who most bitterly resent the American occupation, because under it many of them were deprived of their former wealth or power and some were imprisoned as war criminals. Resentment of our destruction of Japan during the war, even of the atomic bombings, is surprisingly mild, however. The Japanese accept the basic blame for the war.

Beneath the surface of anti-Americanism, moreover, there is an even broader stream of pro-Americanism. Most people personally are extremely friendly to Americans. There is a tacit assumption that high standards prevail in the United States. Even our critics feel that there is more point in leveling their barbs against us than against our opponents, because they assume that Americans are reasonable and likely to act on the basis of principle. The attribution of all the woes of the world to us is in a sense a flattering overestimation of our importance. At the grass-roots level, pro-Americanism runs strong. Everything American—from gadgets to styles and political institutions—is assumed to be better than elsewhere in the world. The common Japanese pays us the most straightforward compliment of all —imitation. Advertisers find it useful to claim popularity for their goods in New York but would hardly be inclined to claim popularity for them in Paris or London, much less in Peking or Moscow.

6. *The Defense Question*

As we have seen, the Japanese in the last few years have been venturing out into international affairs, seeking a role in the world and at the same time trying to define for themselves their "national identity." Japan has been swept recently by a great debate—primarily about foreign policy but also about defense. For the first time since the war, it has become intellectually respectable to discuss military matters. Led by a remarkable group of younger scholars, the Japanese have begun to examine critically and constructively all the old, unquestioned doctrines of both the left and the right, which have been set for twenty years in the concrete of dogma.

Recent events in China have also shaken old preconceptions about that country. Ever since the Communist takeover, most Japanese have striven to see nothing but good in the great Communist experiment next door. This was because of their traditional esteem for Chinese culture, their own loss of self-confidence, the strong influence in Japan of Marxist theories, and the pervasive sense of guilt they had because of the disruptive role Japan had played in China during the previous century. The absurdities of the Cultural Revolution and the Red Guards movement, however, have changed all this. They remind Japanese of the excesses of their own militaristic period, and they reveal how backward China is compared to Japan.

While Japanese attitudes toward China are, at least for

the time being, conflicting and confused, most Japanese agree that they should increase their economic and technological aid to the other less developed countries, especially those of East and Southeast Asia, though how and at what pace this should be done are still matters of debate. A more divisive area of discussion concerns the defense needs of Japan, the future of the American alliance, and the balance of Japan's relations between the Western democracies and the great Communist states.

Most Japanese recognize that Japan's first international interest lies in its relations with the United States and the rest of the advanced Western nations. The United States, as we have seen, provides close to 30 per cent of its total export market as well as imports—a figure that is not at all out of line with America's control of close to one third of the world's wealth. Canada, Australia, and New Zealand account for about 12 per cent of Japan's imports and together with Western Europe take about 18 per cent of her exports. By contrast, trade with all of the Communist countries, after some years of unfettered growth, amounts to only about 6 or 7 per cent of Japan's total trade. Communist nations by nature are not great traders—not the sort of trading partners Japan needs because of its own meager geographic base. Japan's cultural and intellectual contacts also are overwhelmingly with the Western countries, particularly the United States. Its whole modern way of life resembles that of the democratic West more than that of any other part of the world. Without close and warm relations with these countries, Japan would be a lonely orphan indeed.

Nonetheless, the defense ties to the United States are anathema to much of the left and in many ways irksome to more conservative Japanese. Neutralism, unarmed or possibly armed, still seems safer to some than alignment with any military power. The Gaullist approach also has its appeal to Japanese as much as to other peoples. Excessive dependence on the United States is galling to national pride, and some Japanese wonder if Japan must not be militarily strong to play any significant role in the world. Even nuclear weapons have their attraction, at least for prestige purposes.

The debate will undoubtedly continue to swirl along these lines, especially as we come closer to 1970. In the course of the debate, however, certain realities of the situation will probably become clearer to the Japanese public than they now seem to be. Unarmed neutrality obviously is not a realistic policy for a great industrial nation placed geographically where Japan is. It would put Japan's wealth at the mercy of military blackmail from almost any country —nuclear threats, menace to shipping lanes, and the like. On the other hand, armed neutrality or Gaullism would be extremely costly to a country in Japan's position. Sweden, Switzerland, and France all pay heavily for these policies by more than average, rather than less than average, military expenditures. In addition, they have the advantage of being in a stable part of the world, neatly embedded in a large defense alliance, NATO, which actually gives them their chief security, whether they wish to acknowledge this or not. Japan stands all alone as a modern nation in a very unstable part of the world.

A neutral Japan would have to carry a military burden far beyond the 1.2 per cent of the GNP the Japanese have hitherto been devoting to defense. This percentage is well below the average of from 4 to 6 per cent of GNP for countries of similar size and advancement—to say nothing of the roughly 8 to 10 per cent average of the United States, the Soviet Union, and Communist China. Neutralism would cut seriously into Japan's prosperity and the economic role it could play in Asia, and the rearmament it would necessitate would alienate many of its neighbors.

The chief argument for neutralism in Japan is that it would save Japan in the case of a war between the United States and the great Communist powers, but this is specious. China itself is capable of fighting only a localized war, which need not affect Japan in any case, but, if war were to expand to a nuclear conflict between the United States and the Soviet Union, Japan, as an advanced trading nation, would share in the general collapse of world civilization, whatever its alignments might be.

On the other hand, neutralism would lose Japan much of its present security. Defense against invasion from abroad is a minor problem. As a solid island country, Japan is lucky in this respect. The Japanese also could probably build a nuclear umbrella against China's tiny nuclear capacity. They already have developed the rocketry for this, and they possess the nuclear know-how and industrial base to turn out nuclear weapons. But, given the strong pacifism of the public and its special horror of nuclear weapons that stems from the nuclear bombing of Hiroshima and Nagasaki, would such a course be as politically feasible as continuation of the American alliance? In any case, it would give Japan no nuclear deterrent against the Soviet Union. One can only conclude that, because of Japan's narrow geographic base, there really is no alternaitve to the free American deterrence.

More important than the actual defense of Japan itself, however, would be the problem of stability in East Asia and the security of sea lanes, both of which are vital to Japan. These are the main benefits Japan derives from its defense relationship with the United States. Neutralism would mean the end of American bases in Japan and probably in Okinawa also. American bases in Okinawa, to say nothing of American administrative control of the island, would become politically untenable. The loss of these bases would greatly increase the cost and decrease the efficiency of the rest of our military stance in the West Pacific. In particular, it would reduce our ability to offer security to South Korea and maintain the Seventh Fleet at its present strength in the Far East. I also believe it would undermine the American determination to maintain a military posture in the West Pacific. The Vietnam War has done this to a certain extent already. The defection of our chief potential partner in the area and the main beneficiary from our defense policies would be an even greater blow. The only important immediate value to us of our military stance in East Asia is the protection of Japan itself. If this is removed, the American public may not wish to make still greater efforts only for uncertain long-range benefits.

If America gives up its stabilizing role, there will no doubt be a sharp increase in instability throughout Asia and a resultant slowdown of economic growth. Though a blow to hopes for world peace, this would not endanger our immediate interests. It would, however, have immediate adverse effects on Japan. Close to a quarter of its total exports go to non-Communist East and South Asia. Almost half of the energy sources on which it lives—the oil of the Middle East—passes through the Straits of Malacca. If Japan did not wish to cooperate with us in our efforts to promote stability in Asia, Americans, I believe, would be inclined to let the Japanese face these problems alone. The American isolation from the less developed parts of Asia, which I fear in any case as a possible outcome of the Vietnam War, would become very much more probable, and, next to the countries of that area, Japan would be the chief loser.

The Security Treaty is clearly of great benefit to Japan —even greater benefit than it is to the United States. This simple fact, I believe, is beginning to emerge in Japan, as more and more people come to accept it as "common sense." It seems very improbable to me that Japan will seek to break the treaty in 1970, even though the left will no doubt feel committed to putting on a determined demonstration of opposition at that time. It is my guess that the Security Treaty will continue in effect without major modification almost indefinitely, as probably was expected in 1960 when it was first negotiated.

Of course, the actual defense relationship between the

two countries will go on changing, as it has in the past. The American military presence in Japan will continue its downward trend, as the Japanese assume most if not all of the immediate defense of the islands and their near sea and air approaches. The Japanese government has set as a target 2 per cent of GNP for defense, which seems to me quite realistic if the defense alliance with the United States continues.

Okinawa presents a more pressing problem. It is at present very important to the whole American military posture in East Asia and as such is of great value to Japan's own security. A major share of the economy of the islands also depends on our defense expenditures there. At the same time, the nationalistic yearnings of the close to a million Japanese in the Ryukyus and the nationalistic response of their 100 million compatriots in the homeland cannot be ignored in this day and age. So large an "irredenta" inevitably joins the deep feelings of nationalism to the dogma of the left and the passions of anti-Americanism. This is a problem that should be solved quickly, before the crisis of 1970 draws additional fuel from it.

A way must be found to permit the "reversion" of Okinawa to Japan without seriously endangering the security interests of both Japan and the United States. While our extensive bases in Okinawa are deeply entangled in the lives of the local population, means can surely be found to divide the bases from political control. The distance between our somewhat restricted rights in our bases in Japan and our theoretically unencumbered rights in the Okinawa bases is not really very great, especially when one realizes that no major American military effort in the Korean-Chinese-Siberian area would really be possible without Japanese support or at least tacit cooperation. Surely a realistic compromise between the present status of the Okinawan bases and that of the bases in Japan, which would permit the reversion of the Ryukyus, can be reached before 1970—

or at least a fixed date for such a solution. This is in a sense Priority Problem No. 1 between Japan and the United States. The two countries are just too important to each other to allow an issue of this sort to endanger their relationship.

7. *The Future of Our Relations with Japan*

The great debate in Japan over foreign policy, defense, and the American treaty will continue to bubble and boil for the next few years, but I feel reasonably sure of the outcome. We and the Japanese are as natural partners as the United States and Western Europe. Of course, there are greater language barriers and, more seriously, differing cultural backgrounds and contrasting historical experiences. We were the victors and they the vanquished in the Second World War. We are reacting—perhaps overreacting—to the realization that our isolation in the past helped produce the world conditions that led to great and destructive wars. They are reacting—and again probably overreacting—to the realization that their own militarism and imperialism brought them to disaster. The world can look very different from these two contrasting historical vantage points.

Nonetheless, the mutual advantage of close friendship and the fundamental identity of American and Japanese interests in the rest of the world convince me that the United States and Japan will continue to build a relationship with each other much like that between the United States and the United Kingdom. We and the Japanese have the same basic hopes for a peaceful world of diverse but nonaggressive national units living under a rule of law, as symbolized by the United Nations. What we basically want in Asia is what the Japanese desire even more emphatically. We have the same interest in maximizing world trade, only this is of even greater importance to the Japanese than to us. We and they have much the same ideals of a free, democratic society at home. While there is considerable misunderstanding and occasional mistrust, our actual conflicts of interest —fishing rights, airplane routes, and controls over the import of goods and capital—constitute only a trifling fringe of problems in a huge and mutually beneficial relationship.

It is probable that the Japanese, resentful of the long period of actual and then seeming dominance of their foreign relations by the United States, will demand a truly "independent" foreign policy. This is entirely natural and desirable. Japan will be able to do much more of value in the world and to be of more help to us at the same time if she is an independent partner rather than a reluctant follower. We should have no worries about whatever ties she wishes to make with the Soviet Union or China. The inflexibility and suspicions of both, as Communist states, and the Soviet refusal even to consider the return of the southern Kuril Islands, which the Japanese feel are rightly theirs, will probably keep these relations less cordial than might be desirable in the interests of world peace.

Japan's independence of us in the rest of Asia may prove an asset rather than a liability. It will give Japan greater freedom to play the role of bridge between East and West that has already been mentioned. It also may prove a useful counterbalance to us. Our size and power make Asians nervous about us. The presence of a strong and influential Japan in the area may reduce these fears. Similarly, as Japan gains in influence, Asians may begin to worry about its dominance, at which point we become a useful offsetting influence to it. Japan and the United States can probably achieve much more for Asia as two independent forces than if they were united in a leader-follower relationship.

As I see it, the chief problem in American-Japanese relations is that we both tend to take each other too much for granted. The Japanese have assumed that no matter what they do we will continue to play the stabilizing military role in East Asia that we have in the past and also will continue to contribute to Asia's economic development. It has, therefore, seemed convenient to some Japanese to accept the benefits of the American policy while disassociating Japan from any of its costs or dangers. In a sense, these Japanese have wished to continue the international situation of the time of the American occupation, when all international responsibilities did fall on the United States and none on Japan.

We, for our part, have tended to overlook the great importance to us of what Japan is and what role it may play in Asia. While overreacting to very remote or indirect threats to our interests in China and the rest of Asia, we have been somewhat insensitive to how our reactions might affect Japan and our relations with it. Such considerations should be a major factor in determining our policies toward China or Vietnam, but they never have been. Our escalation of the war in Vietnam in 1965 so frightened the Japanese that it clearly delayed their emergence in a more positive role of economic aid and political involvement in Asia. This was detrimental both to our long-range interests and to theirs.

While Japan will continue to depend heavily on our military presence in the Western Pacific, the United States will increasingly depend on Japan's economic cooperation and on its political initiatives in the whole area. We and the Japanese in our own respective interests must consult with each other on major policy problems much more fully than we have in the past and must let our respective policies be more strongly influenced by the other's point of view. This is the only way that we can give each other the mutual support we both need.

We should also be sure that we are treating Japan as a full equal economically. Using the argument that Japanese wages are cheap—an argument that is, incidentally, no longer valid—we have, through "voluntary restrictions," created barriers to Japanese imports that we do not place in the way of trade with the other industrialized nations.

Discrimination of this sort against any of the advanced industrialized countries and particularly against the one that diverges culturally from the others is very unwise.

Actually this problem concerns all the advanced industrialized countries. The future of Japan is proportionately as important to Australia, Canada, New Zealand, and the countries of Western Europe as to us. But they have tended to discriminate against it economically much more than we do. Barriers to Japanese imports, imposed when Japan was a defeated enemy, remain high in Europe. Australia and Canada, while finding a major market in Japan, keep imports from Japan to only a little over half of exports. Although we managed in 1964 to get membership for Japan as the one non-Atlantic member of the OECD (Organization for Economic Cooperation and Development), the economic club of the advanced nations, it has still not been given fully equal economic treatment by the others. Of course, the other side of the coin is that Japan itself should stop its special discriminatory practices against the goods and capital of the United States and the other advanced nations.

In their search for a world role and "national identity," some Japanese wonder if Japan is essentially "Asian" or "Western." If by "Western" they mean "modern," then the answer, of course, is that it is both. That is the true significance of Japan's position. It can play its bridge role only if both ends of the bridge are securely anchored. Its economic, intellectual, and cultural interests lie overwhelmingly in its relations with the advanced Western nations. The firmer that end of the bridge is, the better it will reach across to the other side, where emotion, history, and geographic propinquity pull the Japanese. There is talk in Japan of a Pacific Community consisting of Japan, the United States, Australia, Canada, New Zealand, and, in time, those Asian countries that qualify economically for membership. Such an organization, I feel, would strengthen the "modern" end of the bridge and enhance rather than detract from Japan's role in regional Asian groupings.

In any case, major objectives of America's Asian policy should be to encourage the prosperity and stability of Japan, strengthen its ties of full equality with us and the other modernized countries of the West, and cooperate with it in its growing role of economic aid and bridge-building in Asia. These are all matters of crucial importance to us, for not only is Japan of great significance in itself but our future relationship with all the rest of Asia depends to a very large extent on what Japan becomes and what it does.

II

China

Next to Japan, China looms largest in importance in our relationship with Asia. This is because it has close to half the total population and productive capacity of the rest of East and South Asia. In fact, it has more than one fifth of the world's total population. This huge segment of the human race is under the control of leaders who are violently hostile to us and determined to see their particular political faith and system of organization sweep the world. Thus China constitutes the greatest challenge in Asia and possibly in the whole world to American desires for the future. As Japan embodies our major hopes for Asia, China epitomizes our greatest fears.

1. *The Heritage of the Past*

Our knowledge about China is much less clear than that about Japan. Even the population is a matter of doubt. I believe 700 million is a reasonable estimate, but respectable authorities will give it as anywhere from 650 million to 850 million. Our estimates of its economic productivity are even less certain. Our understanding of the thinking and methods

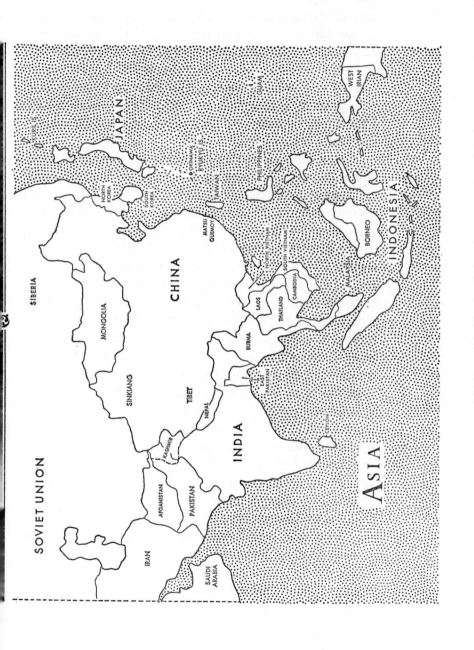

of control of its leadership is at best hazy, and our knowledge of the actual living conditions and attitudes of the people throughout the vast expanse of China is extremely fragmentary. All these uncertainties are compounded by rapid and sometimes bewildering changes in the situation in this still very unstable country. Our focus on China cannot be as sharp as on contemporary Japan. To try to understand what it may be today, we must draw more heavily on our knowledge of its past.

China, which is certainly the oldest still extant political unit in the world, has been for at least the past two millennia the largest in population as well. First unified as a centralized empire in the late third century B.C., it probably had a greater population than that of the Roman Empire, pushed its armies even farther afield, and had at least comparable wealth. We know of no demand for Roman goods in China comparable to the avid demand in Rome for Chinese silks.

Both empires collapsed at about the same time and for somewhat similar reasons. The great difference in the history of Europe and China is that while Rome was never revived, the Chinese Empire had been restored by the seventh century and was stronger and richer than ever. Perhaps the much higher density of the Chinese agricultural population gave it a greater mass and therefore a momentum more resistant to barbarian invasions. Perhaps the Chinese concept of rule by a bureaucracy of merit rather than by an aristocracy of privilege and the sword gave it greater strength for survival at this phase of world history than did the great Roman institution of impersonal law, which has proved so essential to the contemporary world.

In any case, the Chinese Empire, as reconstituted by the seventh century, proved thereafter virtually indestructible. China for the next several centuries was also well ahead of the rest of the world in wealth, technology, and institutional development. It developed a remarkably stable and self-regenerative social and political system, extremely resistant to external pressures and internal erosion.

The Chinese during this long period of unified and stable rule developed a tremendous sense of unity as a culture and as a single political entity. With the help of a uniform system of writing and a written language of great prestige, this unity has transcended differences in spoken tongues, for actually the Chinese of the coastal areas southward from Shanghai speak languages related to but different from that of northern and central China. The Chinese, separated by huge barriers of mountains, deserts, and jungles from the Indian, Islamic, and Western zones of civilization, developed a strong sense of being not just the leading country and civilization in the world, but the only truly civilized land.

All these attitudes still influence the contemporary Chinese. Their country has often been divided into warring states or factions, but all Chinese feel this is not normal. They cannot conceive of a variety of Chinese-speaking nations, as there are many Spanish-speaking or English-speaking countries. The very thought of "two Chinas" is anathema to both Peking and Taipei. Chinese abroad retain their national identity much longer than do emigrants from most other countries. After generations in Southeast Asia, some Chinese communities remain essentially Chinese and are therefore a special problem. Even in the United States before the Second World War, Chinese, with no backing from their confused and divided homeland, entered more slowly into the mainstream of American life than did Japanese, who had behind them an intensely clannish, strongly unified, and violently nationalistic country.

The stability of Chinese society—its perfection in its own terms—made it less responsive to the Western challenge in the nineteenth century. It took repeated massive blows over a long period of time to clear away enough of the magnificent old structure to permit the building of a more modernized one. The long turmoil of this destructive process, coinciding as it did with a period of dynastic decline, gave to Westerners the impression that China was by nature a sloppy, disorganized, almost chaotic country. Actually the organization and regimentation of the Communist period has been more characteristic of Chinese history over the past millennium than the confusion of the century that preceded it.

Chinese pride as the oldest, biggest, and, in their eyes, the only truly civilized nation in the world has made the past century of weakness and humiliation at foreign hands particularly galling. This accounts for the fanatic xenophobia of a China once more reconstituted as a great political unit. It also accounts for some of the radicalism of Chinese ideas. Once the need for a break with tradition became apparent, the Chinese were even more dissatisfied than other peoples with a gradualistic approach that would only slowly overcome China's weakness and relative backwardness. Something more drastic was needed to hurtle China again into the forefront of world civilization. This is part of the appeal of Communism, which by definition puts Communist countries ahead of all others. This is perhaps part of the psychological background that produced the split with the Soviet Union. By proclaiming most of the world hopeless infidels and the Soviet Union and its associates heretics, the Chinese leaders, in their own minds, swept again to the head of the procession, as the only true believers in the only true religion.

2. China's Strength

All this may help explain some of the puzzling attitudes of the Chinese, but more important is the question of China's actual strength and capacity for growth. The very size of the Chinese population has for long caused anxieties in parts of the world. The Germans and other Europeans became exercised over the "yellow peril" half a century or more ago. Some of this attitude seems to linger on among the Russians, who see China's millions pressing against the thinly populated wastes of Siberia.

In actuality, however, China's share of the world population has for long been static or even declining. If present population figures are so uncertain, we cannot be very sure about earlier ones, but it would seem that China's population was a higher percentage of world population a century ago and was almost certainly so a millennium ago. Growing now at around 2 per cent per year, as contrasted to rates averaging closer to 3 per cent in other less developed regions, it may be further losing ground.

In any case, gigantism in population, especially for less developed countries, is probably a source more of weakness than of strength. The larger the social and political unit, the more the effort that must be put into the tasks of unification and coordination. In other words, the organizational overhead will probably be higher, and at the same time there is likely to be greater inefficiency because the same mechanisms of organization and control are sometimes applied to widely divergent situations. Even for an advanced nation like the United States, with its huge reservoir of highly developed skills, this becomes a serious problem. For a less advanced nation, it can be a crushing burden. In this sense, the mere size of both China and India may make these countries clumsy and slow-moving giants, at a distinct disadvantage as compared with smaller but more agile countries. In a way, the nineteenth-century story of the inadequate response to the Western challenge of a cumbersomely ponderous China and the quick-footed response of a smaller Japan may be repeated in more modern form in various parts of Asia.

There are reasons, however, for rating the Chinese

growth potential high. They have a genius for organization and management. How else can one explain their maintenance of the world's largest political unit throughout history, for much of the time at higher levels of efficiency than existed elsewhere in the world? The speed and thoroughness with which the Communists brought peace and order to the whole of China after their takeover in 1949 was a remarkable feat. In a huge and very poor country, disrupted by war and civil strife for most of the past century, they rapidly achieved close political integration and a redistribution of wealth that seems to have eliminated the starvation and beggary that had been endemic for decades.

It could even be argued that the Chinese, together with the other peoples of their zone of civilization—the Japanese, Koreans, and probably the Vietnamese too—have cultural traits that are peculiarly advantageous in today's world. For one thing they have a "northern" culture—that is, they have ethical traits developed in a hostile climate that necessitated purposeful hard work if the cold, bleak winters were to be survived. Over the millennia this sort of climatic conditioning produced habits of energetic work and attitudes of respect for work as a value in itself. These habits and attitudes survived among the Chinese even when they spread to the subtropical south of China and on into tropical Southeast Asia. They were also transmitted to the Vietnamese, who live in an entirely tropical environment.

The habits and attitudes toward work of East Asian civilization contrast with the emphasis on relaxation, amusement, and meditation, which are sensible responses to climates that are more generous with food the year round and make overly hard work physically dangerous at some times of the day or year. The cultural contrast with South Asia, Africa, and Latin America is marked. In some ways there may even be a contrast with our own Western culture, because for us modern technology has over a longer period of time somewhat relaxed the necessity for incessant work and therefore may have weakened our enthusiasm for it. East Asians still retain capacities for work that help account for Japan's rapid rise and give a promise of growth to both China and Korea, and possibly Vietnam, that some less developed countries do not have.

An even more important East Asian characteristic for the future may be the enthusiasm for learning. Possibly because of the unparalleled difficulty of writing systems based on the thousands of complicated Chinese characters, there developed in East Asia a greater respect for writing and literacy than in any other of the great civilizations and a stronger popular desire for book learning. Again, these attitudes lie behind the high literacy rates of Japan in the middle of the nineteenth century and its success in achieving full literacy some decades ago. They are reflected in the high rates of university attendance in the countries of East Asia—far beyond the levels their economies would explain. They can be seen in the level of university education among Americans of East Asian ancestry—a higher level than that of any other ethnic group. In the modern age, in which high levels of scientific and technological knowledge are so important for economic growth, this popular esteem for education and great desire for learning are national assets of inestimable value. Again the contrast is sharp with most other less developed parts of the world.

Because of their strong drives for hard work and learning and their unexcelled skills at organization, which at least in part offset the disadvantage of gigantism, the distant, long-range future of the Chinese may be relatively promising, but we are more concerned with their more immediate prospects at this unstable moment in world history. What has the record been in Communist China? The achievements during most of the first decade of Communist rule were impressive. Not only did the Communists restore a high degree of political order in their hitherto war-torn and demoralized land but their economy also moved ahead at a tremendous pace. Chinese statistics are too uncertain to be worth quoting, but there can be no doubt that the rate of economic growth during these years was faster than in India or most of the rest of Asia. China's prestige rose throughout the less developed world, and its threat by example loomed even larger than its threat by subversion or military aggression. These were the years when Americans became terrified that a great Communist wave would sweep out of China over most of Asia.

Since then, however, the picture has changed radically. For almost a decade China has been in the economic doldrums. The rapid growth of the first decade may have been in large part the natural result of the restoration of peace, order, and unity to the whole of continental China for the first time in many generations. It may have been more an administrative than an economic achievement, and Communist systems of organization proved very efficient for this. Since then the Chinese have faced the problems of new economic growth on the basis of the recovery resulting from restored unity. For this, Communist methods have proved less successful. The Soviet model did not do well under the more backward conditions of China, and, when the Chinese Communists tried innovations of their own, there were outright disasters.

The time of troubles started after 1956 when Mao Tse-tung, assuming that he had remade the minds of his people more than he had, encouraged the blooming of "a hundred flowers" of divergent opinion. The resulting flood of criticism in the spring of 1957 was more than he had counted on, and he quickly cut down the "flowers" that had appeared and resumed the old totalitarian controls. Then later that same year, restive with the Soviet pattern of economic development, Mao called for a "great leap forward." Remembering how his Communist movement, in its rise to power, had overcome all obstacles by mustering the support of the Chinese masses, he tried to make China surge forward economically by a massive use of its greatest resource—the hard work of its 700 million people. He hoped that by enthusiasm and fanatic effort, the Chinese people could climb to new economic levels.

It did not work that way. Economic growth in the modern world requires not just hard work and capital investment, but also careful coordination and the development of technical skills. These elements were sadly deficient. Efforts at producing steel in back-yard furnaces, for example, proved extremely wasteful of resources as well as manpower. The economy got completely out of kilter. Transportation was disrupted. The attempt to communize agriculture through large factory-like communes, started in the summer of 1958, undermined old patterns of work and so reduced personal incentives that there was a drastic drop in output. China, with 80 per cent of its working force still in agriculture, became unable to feed itself and was forced to import large quantities of wheat from the "capitalist" West.

The story is a complex and confused one. Adverse weather conditions probably played a part. The termination of large-scale Soviet aid in 1959 and 1960 also had an influence. This termination was not just the result of the Chinese divergence from Soviet economic precepts but more the product of the underlying rivalry between the Chinese and Russians, and it may have been triggered by Soviet reluctance to support China's development of nuclear weapons. The full story may never be known, but the economic disaster was obvious. China, instead of leaping forward economically, slid backward for a while. The government had to withdraw from the full communization of agriculture in order to avoid even more serious food deficits. By backtracking in such ways, it stopped the economic decline and began to move the country ahead again, but more slowly than before. Foreign trade by 1966 had still not recovered fully to its 1959 level, and the overall rate of growth for China since 1959 has been well below that of many of its neighbors. Thus in proportionate terms China has shrunk in size.

Today we are witnessing another convulsion in China. Mao and his supporters, or at least those who act in his name, still appear to be dissatisfied with China's faltering economic pace and to be even more concerned over the apparent decline of revolutionary zeal among the people and the bureaucracy. Still confident of their ability to remake human nature and, as they see it, "liberate" human energy, they once again seem to be seeking to solve China's problems through stirring up mass enthusiasm. They fear the development of an entrenched bureaucracy as a conservative force and wish to guard against this by having the youth of China experience revolutionary struggle.

An entrenched bureaucracy, however, does exist not only in the government and in industry but also in the Communist Party itself, and many of these bureaucrats remember the disasters of the "great leap forward," when faith once before was put in the efficacy of mass enthusiasm. A deepening cleavage apparently has developed between those who take the more conservative and pragmatic approach of seeking economic progress and national strength through the accumulation of technical skills and careful coordination by bureaucratic administrative controls and those who look back to the old technique of mobilizing mass energy. The argument may have been sharpest in the military field between those who advocate a truly professional army with modern weapons and those who put their faith in decentralized guerrilla strategy.

There are, of course, other facets to the turmoil in China. It seems in part a power struggle between individuals and groups. Possibly Mao's fading physical condition has sparked a fight over the succession. We know too little about what goes on at the higher levels in Peking to be sure. In any case, however, there is also a rancorous division between the experts and those who look back to the techniques of the old guerrilla days. The Maoists have described the difference as being between the true revolutionaries and the "revisionists" who would permit a return to "bourgeois" ethics and even "capitalism." A truer description would probably be of a division between technicians and bureaucrats on the one side and political zealots on the other, or between pragmatists and visionaries—between those who would rather be fed than red, at least red in Mao's particular shade.

To prepare the ground for the new effort, the Maoists launched in the spring of 1966 their Cultural Revolution, designed apparently to eliminate the doubters or browbeat them into silence. When it proved less than fully successful, they adopted a technique that seems all but incredible in a totalitarian country. They mobilized the youth of China into Red Guard bands, which were meant to sweep away the opposition entrenched in the organs of government and the Communist Party. Virtually a whole year of schooling was sacrificed to the effort—a terrible price in a country still so deficient in education.

The results at the time of this writing are inconclusive. Much damage must have been done to the whole machine of government and party administration. After the wave of denunciations and kangaroo courts, middle-level administrators, whether factory managers or college presidents, will be much more hesitant than before to show the leadership that is needed. The Red Guards proved a rather heavy, blunt instrument for a delicate political operation. They spread much confusion, and at times groups of them came to blows with one another. A great deal of disillusionment will undoubtedly follow the early euphoria of the movement. The myth of absolute unity and unerring wisdom of the Communist leadership has been shattered. Another economic downturn could follow. At the very least, economic growth has once again been slowed.

Almost anything could still happen. My personal guess, however, is that the disruption caused by the Cultural Revolution and Red Guards movement will be held in bounds. The Chinese have great skills for compromise as well as organization. All the leaders are firm believers in Communism, even if they differ in methods of approach to their immediate problems. The army, as the locus of ultimate power, may play a growing role that helps stabilize the situation. Still, the past year and a half of turmoil in China is all the more reason for believing that economic progress will continue to be slow for a while. The Communists obviously have no magic formula for growth in a country like China. The Chinese may do well to average an excess of 1 to 3 per cent in economic growth over population growth. In other words, they will continue to fall behind Japan and most of the rest of the industrialized world. They may also continue to be outpaced by South Korea, Taiwan, Thailand, Malaysia, Pakistan, and some of their other neighbors.

In the brilliant success of the Chinese Communists in restoring political order and their record of only modest economic growth, we may have a repetition of an old Chinese story. In the past, the early years of a successful dynasty always witnessed the establishment of firm political control over the country and, as a result of peace and order, a rapid restoration of the economy destroyed by the years of turmoil that had brought the previous dynasty down. In their desire to fill the imperial treasury with a maximum flow of taxes and to control society so that revolution would be impossible, most dynasties established very rigid economic controls and tended to tax to death any very promising enterprise. As a result, periods of strong rule were usually times of little real economic growth. Only when the dynasties had started to decline and had been forced to relax their grip on the people was there ever much economic innovation and growth. Then the genius of the Chinese people for economic activity was allowed to express itself. How great this genius is can be seen from what Chinese have achieved under the less binding grip of the colonial regimes of Southeast Asia and Hong Kong or again in the freer society of Hawaii and the continental United States. There is reason to believe that the Chinese Communists are repeating the old dynastic story of strangling the goose of Chinese economic genius before it can lay its golden eggs. Perhaps a much less totalitarian form of government is needed if the Chinese people are to achieve the economic progress of which they are capable.

3. China's Threat

Even an economically slow-moving China, however, is still a huge unit, has the largest army in the world, and evinces frightening hostility toward us and most other countries. What is its threat to world peace and to the security of its neighbors?

China's military power is, I believe, unbeatable—on Chinese soil. Despite the recent disorders, there seems little likelihood that the Communist grip on the nation will be loosened. The regime may be doing poorly in economic growth and may be disliked by the people for many specific reasons, but conditions in many respects are enough better today than they were over most of the past century that Communist prestige, no doubt, remains high among the people. The country is not likely to break up into regions at war with one another. China's cohesiveness and the organizational skills of its people are too great to make this probable. Even if the country should drift toward such chaotic conditions, the people would, no doubt, remain united against any threat of outside domination. The huge population mobilized in guerrilla warfare could absorb and neutralize any outside military power, and Chinese pride would probably stand firm even against the threat of nuclear destruction.

China's huge forces of foot soldiers also can be formidable in areas near China's borders to which they can walk. We discovered this in North Korea. We will find the story repeated if we tangle with Chinese armies in North Vietnam. Chinese soldiers could keep guerrilla wars going almost indefinitely in Southeast Asia, if the local people were to call them in and support them. This would be a form of escalation of the Vietnam War that could prove disastrous to us.

There are sharp limitations, however, to the geographic extent of Chinese military power. China simply does not have the industrial base to fight the kind of war the Japanese fought a quarter of a century ago, when they destroyed our naval power and defeated Western armies some 3,000 miles from their own home bases. China has virtually no navy and does not have the industry and technology to build or maintain a first class fleet or air force. Its deficiencies in transportation would make even its land armies relatively ineffective in hostile terrain far from home. They would be as vulnerable to guerrilla harassment as any other foreign army and less able to maintain their lines of supply. Because of our great mobility by air and sea and China's poor transport capacity even by land, the United States is strategically much closer to many parts of East and South Asia than is China. It is for these reasons that any attempt by China to conquer and hold down India or much of Southeast Asia would prove disastrous for China.

China's development since 1964 of a small nuclear capacity has not, in my judgment, notably changed the military equation. Large nuclear arsenals have produced a balance of terror in the world but have not proved usable, because even a small use of nuclear weapons may trigger a nuclear holocaust that would destroy both sides. How much less useful is a tiny nuclear arsenal—and for the foreseeable future China's potential should be thought of as a hundredth or a thousandth that of the United States or the Soviet Union. Would even a weak neighbor be seriously intimidated by a Chinese nuclear threat, when everyone realizes that the actual use of nuclear weapons by China might bring down on it a much larger nuclear response by us, by the Soviet Union, or possibly by both?

I suspect that the Chinese leaders are perfectly aware of this fact. I would assume, therefore, that they have diverted much of their advanced scientific and engineering skills and an appreciable part of their national wealth to developing nuclear weapons not because they felt that this would give them a chance to dominate their neighbors, but because they believed it would give them a little more security against us. We, with our more generous estimate of our own good sense, may look upon the diversion of so much of China's economic capacity to the production of nuclear weapons as a tragic waste of resources by a poor country. To them, it probably represents a wise investment in security, because they feel that "capitalistic" America is longing to attack them and that even a small Chinese nuclear arsenal may help deter this attack. Thus, their possession of nuclear weapons may serve to relax their fears of us more than it increases their actual menace to others.

Chinese rhetoric is extremely bellicose, but their actions have tended to be cautious. We have seen how their participation in the Korean War seemed to them to be purely defensive and how even the border war with India was not aggression from their point of view. Even with a large-scale war raging on their southern borders in Vietnam, they have, as of the present writing, injected only some 40,000 engineer troops into North Vietnam, in contrast to more than ten times that number of actual combatants whom we have dispatched all the way across the Pacific. Their ruthless conquest of Tibet was to them merely rounding out what they considered to be the traditional territories of China. For more than a thousand years the Chinese have considered Tibet to be a part of their domains, and during recent centuries they actually have dispatched officials and troops to control it.

It might be well to analyze the difference in attitudes of the Chinese toward areas that they have come to regard as traditionally part of their empire and those that they considered to be merely tributary states. Many Americans, confusing the two, think of Southeast Asia as somehow rightfully or inevitably a Chinese zone of influence. This, I feel, is a serious error and a grave injustice to the people of that part of the world.

There is a myth that the Chinese throughout history have been a more pacifistic people than others, but this simply is not true. They did not glorify soldiers, as the feudal Japanese or we in the West did. The sensible Chinese tried to avoid military service. The Chinese Empire, however, was throughout history a large, even if not always efficient, fighting machine. It started draft armies more than two millennia ago. Military service was considered part of the tax burden the common citizen bore. Strong dynasties always conquered far afield. As with other empires, foreign conquests were primarily justified as necessary for security at home. A dangerous borderland had to be subjugated, and to keep it secure the next borderland beyond it would have to be pacified. Chinese armies thus moved outward in conquest, until the lengthening supply line weakened their punch. Since the threat to China traditionally came from the treeless lands of the nomads to the north and west of China, not from the sedentary inhabitants of the jungles and agricultural lands to the south, Chinese conquest went in those directions rather than southward.

At times of strong dynasties, therefore, Chinese armies regularly subjugated Sinkiang (Chinese Turkestan) and parts of Mongolia, Tibet and Manchuria. Under the last dynasty, that of the Manchus, who seized Peking in 1644, all of these lands and even parts of Siberia came under Chinese military control. Chinese came to think of all these areas as rightfully parts of the Chinese Empire and showed them as such on their maps, even though these lands were inhabited for the most part by non-Chinese peoples, except for Manchuria, which was filled up with Chinese only during the past century. It is for this reason that both Peking and Taipei are not happy that, with Russian support, Mongolia (the region formerly known as Outer Mongolia) now ranks as an independent nation.

Korea also was frequently conquered by Chinese armies up until the seventh century and North Vietnam (Tonkin) until the tenth, but thereafter they drifted into the broader category of tributary states. This category included any country that wished to carry on officially recognized trade with China. The Ryukyu Islands were such a tributary state, even when closely ruled from Japan. Japan itself at certain periods before the sixteenth century fitted into the pattern. So did most of the states of Southeast Asia, some parts of India, and states even farther afield. According to Chinese records, Portugal, Holland, and other European lands were at times tributary states of China.

Chinese military power and political control, however, were rarely extended to any of these "tributary" areas. Only under the Mongol rulers of China in the thirteenth century were serious efforts made to conquer Southeast Asia and Japan—and these failed. Later, in the early fifteenth century, the Chinese sent great fleets into Southeast Asia and around to India and the eastern coast of Africa. China was on the point of discovering Europe. The undertaking, however, seemed profitless to the Chinese, and they gave it up. Not since then has China made any effort to control any part of Southeast Asia by military power, except for a few brief punitive expeditions. The growth from the sixteenth century on of the Western colonial empires showed conclusively that China exerted no political power in the area. In the six-teenth and early seventeenth centuries, Japanese merchants and adventurers actually played a more direct military and political role in the countries of Southeast Asia than did the Chinese Empire. Chinese merchants and immigrants in-creasingly found Southeast Asia a fertile area for their eco-nomic activities, but this was not under the protection of China but under the wing of Western colonial regimes.

There are now sizable numbers of Chinese in Southeast Asia, and some experts feel that, because of their great eco-nomic influence as the merchants and middlemen of the region, China will increasingly come to dominate the area, but I suspect that, on the whole, the Chinese in Southeast Asia will have the contrary effect. In Singapore they do constitute the bulk of the population and in Malaya (the continental part of Malaysia) about 40 per cent, but in neither area do they regard themselves politically as part of China. In countries like Thailand, where over a long period of time Chinese immigrants have been absorbed into the mainstream of national life, the new currents of nationalism are, if anything, accelerating this process. In countries like Indonesia and Vietnam, where the Chinese have not been accepted into the mainstream, their power is declining and their continued presence exacerbates feelings against China. Indonesian suspicion of Chinese support for the local Com-munists was, no doubt, greatly increased by strong resent-ment of the economic power of the 2 to 3 per cent of the population that is of Chinese origin. The brutal attacks on the Communists were accompanied by pogroms against the Chinese communities. The Chinese of Southeast Asia are respectable, hard-working people who are to be pitied rather than feared. History is moving against them, and their influence is now basically a negative one, heightening local fears of China and resistance against its possible domi-nation.

Today, with the tides of nationalism running strong

throughout Asia, it seems absurd to regard Southeast Asia as a natural zone of Chinese domination. Japanese and Western economic influences far outclass anything China is capable of extending to this region. Most important, the local people are determined to remain free of domination by any outsiders. This is true even in Communist North Vietnam. If colonialism, with its tolerance for the Chinese interloper, had continued for another century, possibly all of Southeast Asia would in time have been absorbed through Chinese immigration and economic penetration. Under nationalistic regimes, the tides are now flowing in the opposite direction, and most of the area (all except Singapore and possibly Malaysia) seems to have been saved for the indigenous people.

Another distinction should be made between what China did in Tibet and what it can do in South Asia. Tibet is a treeless, thinly populated territory, containing not more than two million people—not a jungle-girt, densely populated region that lends itself to guerrilla warfare. Trying to extend to much of South Asia the iron-fisted control China has established in Tibet would be militarily out of the question.

Actually the Chinese have not shown much eagerness to spread their faith by conquest beyond their traditional borders. They loudly proclaim the necessity of sweeping the world with "wars of national liberation," but they expect this to be done by the local people in each country. They are ready to help stir up these wars and supply their allies with support to the extent of their ability, but they have not shown any desire to fight these wars themselves. In a sense, they are offering a do-it-yourself kit for revolutions.

Some people, while agreeing on this point for the past, feel that the Chinese leaders may embark on military adventures abroad in the future, if they become increasingly irrational or are forced to try to cover up internal dissension by starting wars abroad. I doubt this. The Chinese Communists have for so long used the foreign menace to strengthen unity at home that very little additional strength could be drawn from this strategem, and the greatly increased burden placed by a foreign war on an already overburdened country might increase rather than decrease internal dissension. Moreover, the Chinese leaders, though absurdly wrong on many matters, are not, in my opinion, irrational. Given their basic assumptions and their own personal experiences, they are acting in entirely rational, even coldly calculating, ways. Misunderstanding us and our assumptions, as they do, they probably feel we are as irrational as they appear to us. I would assume that the Chinese leaders will continue to be violent in their statements but cautious and, by their standards, pragmatic in their actions abroad. They may well be drawn into the war in Vietnam, but I would not expect them to indulge suddenly in a burst of military adventurism abroad.

China's greatest threat, I feel, has been and will continue to be not a military threat but a more subtle one of example, of incitement to subversion, and of support to insurgency. The Burmese are so cautious in their relations with us and so fearful of China not because they assume that Chinese armies will roll across their frontiers, though this could happen, but because they have Communist movements within their territories that draw inspiration and probably support from China. The flurry of fear about China in Africa a few years ago was because of efforts by small groups of Chinese there to stir up revolutions. In Indonesia, China's menace was its support of the local Communist movement.

Fortunately, this more real aspect of the Chinese threat has declined markedly in the past few years. China of late has done so poorly at home that it is no longer a very attractive model. Its own ineptness has contributed to the decline of its influence. The Chinese attack on India seriously undercut the whole Communist movement in India and turned a hitherto friendly country into one of China's most bitter enemies. Africans, having carried through their own "revolution" against colonialism, did not appreciate having the Chinese trying to import a new brand of "revolution." Chinese arrogance and their strong racial feelings also could not be permanently concealed and in time stirred up bitter resentments. Although they may not realize it themselves, the Chinese, the Japanese, and many other Asian peoples are as strongly racist in their basic feelings as any people in the world.

China also lacks the economic power to exert much influence through trade or aid. Africans and others have been disappointed by China's inability to make useful contributions to their development. China's foreign trade is less than a quarter of Japan's alone. The relatively expensive foodstuffs it exports in exchange for cheaper foods imported from the West have little appeal for other less developed countries. The products of light industry China can also export are exactly the sort of thing other less developed areas can best produce, and some of them, such as Hong Kong, Taiwan, and Korea, do so better than mainland China. Thus in the economic field, as well as in the military and political fields, China probably has less capacity to dominate other parts of Asia than seemed to be the case a few years ago. Over the long run, of course, the Chinese, with their unusual capacities for hard work, learning, and organization, can come to exert great influence on other areas, but such a situation is still a long time off.

4. American Policy Toward China

The size, antiquity, and mystery of China have always exerted a strong pull on the American imagination. As a result we have tended to overemphasize China's importance to us. The lure of the rich Canton trade first drew Americans to the Far East, and Perry's opening of Japan some six decades later was, in a sense, a mere by-product of our interest in this China trade. Our chief diplomatic efforts continued to be devoted to maintaining the territorial integrity of China and the "open door" for us to its markets long after Japan had replaced China as our chief trading partner in that part of the world. Americans remained bemused with the parallel dream of finding "400 million customers" in China and converting this vast nation to Christianity, at a time when our real problems in the area were our own colonial involvement in the Philippines and our growing clash of interests with the Japanese.

During the Second World War we declared the shaky, dictatorial regime of Chiang Kai-shek to be our "great sister Republic." At the close of the war we insisted that China should be given permanent membership in the Security Council of the United Nations as one of the great stabilizing forces of the world, overlooking the obvious fact that it faced inevitable civil war and would be more a disturber of world stability than a maintainer of it for some time to come. When the Communists won the civil war, we shifted our image of China from hundreds of millions of would-be customers, potential converts, or fellow "republicans" to the now 700 million "enemies" who were to be blamed for almost every problem of instability in Asia. We have never shown much sense of proportion in our dealings with China and still suffer from a special astigmatism when looking at it.

China is indeed a giant, but we have always assumed that it casts a much longer shadow on the world and on our interests than it actually does. We have tended to react to our concept of the shadow rather than to the actual conditions of the giant, mired in part by its own bulk in a slough of backwardness and poverty. We have based our policies on assumptions that the giant was stronger and far more agile than it actually is, when the real long-range problem may well be its weakness and therefore its inability to extricate itself from the unhappy position it has fallen into. Our policy of late has tended to be negative toward China, when we should have been trying to accentuate the positive.

Our negative attitude toward China is easy enough to explain. Having overestimated China's promise and having developed unrealistic hopes about it, we were all the more disappointed, even outraged, when the Chinese turned to Communism and, in part because of our support for the defeated side in the civil war, became violently hostile to us. We felt the jilted lover. Moreover, the Chinese Communists rebuffed our tentative efforts at establishing contacts. Then, their intervention in the Korean War convinced Americans that they were "the enemy" *par excellence.* This relationship—or rather lack of it—froze into the posture still maintained a decade and a half later. It is high time that we now reconsider whether this rigid stance best serves American interests.

Our containment policy has, I believe, been wise and still remains necessary. China is much larger than most of its neighbors, and its leaders are fanatically devoted to the proposition that revolution must be spread throughout the world. We had to hold back Chinese armies in Korea when they came out to meet us after we had made what now seems in retrospect the mistake of crossing the 38th parallel into North Korea. Throughout the 1950's, when Chinese prestige was high, in part because of their ability to hold us to a military stalemate in Korea, China did constitute a serious threat to her neighbors—by intimidation if not by aggression—and therefore our military presence in the area did play a useful role in supporting other Asian countries against this pressure. An American military commitment to some of them may have been necessary for this purpose, though the pretense through SEATO of a full military alliance of many powers, when the only real military strength was the American commitment, was probably not the best way to achieve this.

Even today, with China's prestige fallen far below where it was a decade ago, our military presence is still probably desirable as a warning against open aggression across national frontiers. In a sense, we have a containment policy against aggression throughout the world. In view of China's bellicose stance, there is good reason for us to focus this policy particularly on it—even though open aggression does not seem to be its strategy, at least at present.

There has been a great deal more, however, to our frozen China policy that is less in our interests. We have all this time accepted Chiang Kai-shek's pretense that the civil war in China has not yet been decided and that the Republic of China on Taiwan is the only true Chinese government and will presumably someday recover the mainland. This, of course, is absurd. Chiang controls less than 2 per cent of the Chinese population. However disillusioned the Chinese people may be with their Communist masters, older Chinese probably remain equally disillusioned with Chiang's rule, and younger Chinese have been indoctrinated to look upon Chiang only with contempt. Even if the Communist regime should fall apart on the mainland, which seems improbable, Chiang's regime is not likely to be the beneficiary. History does not often run backward in that way.

No one really thinks that the Republic of China is the government of China. Not only do we seem silly to the rest of the world for seeming to accept this pretense, but the sham puts us from the start in a very disadvantageous position in trying to work out our relationship with this largest single block of humanity. In diplomacy, as well as everything else in life, falsehoods do not offer firm footing.

To maintain the game, we have, of course, refused to consider recognizing Peking and, year after year, have expended great effort to induce others to withhold recognition or at least to join us in blocking Peking's admission to the

United Nations. Many of our allies in the advanced world have refused to go along with us on this, and in none of them is the public basically in sympathy with our policy. In much of the rest of the world there is strong criticism. We have paid a heavy political price for our effort to blackball Peking in world society—a policy which, so far as I can see, has no advantages for us in any case.

Our reasons for this policy seem to me largely specious. Recognition normally is based on the effective control of a country by a regime, not on a moral judgment of its merits, as has been the American approach from time to time in the past half century. We argue that the Peking regime is not fit to be recognized as the government of China. If we were to apply the same moral yardstick elsewhere in the world, we should withdraw recognition from a great number of other countries too. We also argue that Peking does not have the support of the Chinese people, as expressed through free elections. This yardstick would, of course, force withdrawal of recognition from all the nondemocratic countries of the world, which are greatly in the majority and include the government on Taiwan. Actually, if by some miracle free elections were to be held suddenly throughout the world, the Peking regime, I suspect, would come out at least as well as most nondemocratic governments.

Another argument has been that unless we remained firm in refusing to recognize that the Communists control mainland China some of its neighbors would become so dispirited that they would no longer attempt to maintain their independence of China. If these neighbors, however, were in reality so weak-kneed and prized their independence so little, there is nothing we could do in the long run to maintain their independence for them. This argument, I feel, amounts virtually to blackmail by countries that find it to their interests for us not to recognize the existence of Communist China.

Another argument has been that if Peking were admitted to the United Nations and particularly if it were to assume the permanent Chinese seat in the Security Council, the U.N. would be seriously disrupted. Leaving aside the question of whether Peking would be willing to join except on terms unacceptable to the U.N., there is some plausibility to this argument. Chinese intransigence might well prove upsetting to the smooth functioning of the U.N. It seems doubtful, however, that the U.N. actually is now playing much of a peace-keeping role for the Chinese to disrupt. For the most part the U.N. is still more of a hope than a reality.

Moreover, the non-Western countries have placed their hopes heavily on the U.N., and if Peking were to obstruct its work, their indignation, which is now focused on us for blackballing the largest non-Western country, would shift to the Chinese. The bullheadedness Peking would probably show in the U.N. would, no doubt, further sour the other less developed countries on China and thus lessen rather than enhance its prestige. The participation of the Chinese Communists in the U.N. would also be instructive for them, as it would bring them in closer contact with the attitudes and realities of the outside world. This process of educating Peking would probably be of much greater value to the United States than would the disruptive role of Peking in the U.N. be a menace to our interests.

Our refusal to trade with China and our efforts to discourage trade between it and other non-Communist nations have probably also worked against our interests. Our argument has been that China is an aggressive nation and that trade with it, by strengthening its economy, permits it to be all the more aggressive. On the surface this sounds plausible, but actually things have not worked out this way.

This policy might have made sense of a sort if our major allies had been willing to join in a trade embargo, but they have not. Even if they had been willing to join us in boycotting China, the squeeze this would have placed on the Chinese economy might not have had the desired effect. Very likely it would have forced China back into the arms of the Soviet Union, thus restoring some degree of unity in the Communist world. From this point of view, trade between China and the non-Communist nations is basically to our advantage. It helps make possible the continued division of the Communist world and, by letting the Chinese become dependent on trade with non-Communist nations, may help induce them in time to accept peaceful coexistence with the rest of us. In any case, it seems improbable that even a total trade embargo by the non-Communist countries would have appreciably reduced China's capacity to stir up revolutions in less developed countries and to give the sort of aid in small arms and engineering troops that it is presently providing North Vietnam.

The essential point, however, is that all of our major allies do trade freely with Communist China. It is true that they have banned trade in items of strategic importance and have agreed to limit long-term credits, saving economic aid of this sort for countries that seem more deserving, but efforts by us to force them to stop normal commercial contacts with China would only damage our relations with them. With the exception of the Soviet Union, which ranks third in China's trade, Peking's chief trading partners constitute the roster of our major allies. In descending order of importance they are Japan, the United Kingdom (through its Hong Kong colony), West Germany, France, Canada, Australia, and Italy. More than 70 per cent of China's trade is done with the non-Communist world.

Under these circumstances our own refusal to trade with China has had no economic effect at all. China already has far more markets for her goods and sources of supply for her needs than her weak economy can exploit. The meaninglessness in economic terms of our embargo is illustrated by the export of wheat by the United States and Canada to Japan and China. In recent years, some of the Canadian wheat that had been going in large quantities to Japan began to flow to China instead, thus opening up a corresponding share of the Japanese market to our wheat. China's economy and even the size and nature of its external trade have not been influenced by our trade policies but have been determined primarily by internal conditions and China's changing relations with the Soviet Union. These have developed the way they have more despite than because of American policies.

Our trade embargo may have had no economic effect, but, together with our refusal to recognize Peking and our frantic efforts to keep it out of the U.N., it has had political effects, and these basically have been contrary to our interests. Our whole effort to keep China weak and uninfluential by isolating it has met with little success. We have not been able to cut down on China's economic relations with the outside world. No important country has been inhibited from establishing those contacts with China it judged desirable. Our efforts account for China's absence from the U.N. no more than do its own intransigent actions and unreasonable conditions for membership. China's ability to stir up mischief abroad has not been appreciably lessened. On the other hand, our policy has had an adverse effect on our relations with our allies. In Japan, for example, where China policy looms large and our efforts to isolate it seem unwise to the general public, it has been a major cause of strain in our relations.

Our policy has also contributed to China's hostility toward us and perhaps to the unreasonableness of its stance toward the whole non-Communist world. It should, of course, be recognized that the Chinese Communists would almost certainly have developed a strong hostility toward us no matter what we did. It is an article of faith with them that American "imperialism" is the inevitable product of our "capitalistic" system and is the great enemy of mankind.

Moreover, to cement solidarity at home and gloss over the disappointments of their rule, they needed a foreign enemy, and we admirably fitted the bill. I do not see, however, why we should help them in this game, particularly now that they have found in the Russians a fine substitute for us as Public Enemy No. 1.

The chief argument against our policy of trying to isolate China, however, is that it stands as a massive barrier we ourselves have erected in the way of what must be our long-range goal. China will not wither and blow away; nor is the Communist regime likely to be dislodged in the foreseeable future. Our only reasonable hope is that the Chinese leaders will slowly come to understand the realities of the world around them and begin to see that only through peaceful coexistence with the non-Communist nations and eventually cooperation with them will they be able to achieve the secure and reasonably prosperous China they hope to build. This, of course, may take a very long time, and until it happens, China will probably remain the greatest threat to world stability, keeping the Asian half of the world on edge and nullifying efforts at worldwide agreements on nuclear weapons and other crucial matters. Still, slow though it may be in coming, this is our best hope with regard to China.

It is not surprising that the Chinese leaders are sadly ignorant of the rest of the world. For the most part, they have led very isolated lives. Mao, emerging from the heart of central China, had a brief experience as a young man in the heady international atmosphere of Peking University, where he became a convert to Communist doctrines of the 1920's. Soon, however, he was back in the remote interior, leading his guerrilla movement first in the mountain fastnesses of the southeast and then in the semideserts of the northwest. Geographic isolation together with the blinders of Communist dogma narrowed his vision of the world.

China's tragedy today, as a century ago, is the ignorance

of its leaders regarding the rest of the world. We should be doing all we can to get them in touch with what lies outside China, opening windows for them rather than trying to keep them closed. Until they know more about the realities of the rest of the world, they are not likely to adopt the live-and-let-live philosophy that is necessary for China and for the rest of us.

The irony of the present situation is that we can hardly expect the Chinese to accept this philosophy if we do not seem ready for it ourselves. We may have had our own traumatic shock when China, on which we had placed such high but unrealistic hopes, turned Communist. They, however, are burdened with much heavier psychological problems. It is they rather than we who are weak and backward. They are probably the proudest people in the world and may still find it difficult to accept the rest of us as equals, but they have just lived through a century in which people like us were able to trample almost at will on their pride. Our pretense that they do not really exist, or, if they do, are morally so bad that their existence should be ignored, rubs on raw nerves. Neither Chinese hostility to us nor the basic Chinese threat to world stability was created by our policies, but our policies do much to strengthen and maintain both.

5. *Our Future Stance Toward China*

Much of what I have said above is recognized in Washington and by the American people. Of late we have been moving cautiously away from our earlier attempts to isolate China. For some years now we have not sought to discourage normal trade in nonstrategic goods between our allies and China. We have started to experiment with the description of our policy as "containment without isolation." President Johnson has spoken of "reconciliation" with

China. We have expressed a willingness to exchange news-papermen, scholars, doctors, scientists, and others, without so far having drawn any favorable response from the other side.

There is a reluctance, however, to go beyond these tiny steps to a forthright redefinition of our whole stance on China that would be consistent with the actual situation and with what we really think. We have not been willing to state simply and clearly that we recognize that the Peking government effectively controls virtually all of China and assume that it will continue to do so; that we, therefore, look forward to the time when Peking will be willing to establish normal diplomatic relations with us; that we would be ready to enter into trade relations with it; that we look forward to the time when China will wish to join the United Nations on the same basis on which other countries have joined; and finally that we hope for the time when China will wish to have, not just normal diplomatic contact with us, but friendly and cooperative relations. All these things are definitely in our interest, and there is no reason why we should not state that this is what we wish to see happen.

There are several objections, however, that are frequently raised against doing so. It is argued that, however wise this course may be in the long run, the Vietnam War makes it impossible for us to follow it now. We are told that statements such as these cannot be made while we are fighting "Chinese aggression" in Vietnam. This, however, is a complete misreading of the facts. As we have seen, the war in Vietnam should not be regarded as even an indirect product of Chinese aggression. It is the product of local conditions and some bad choices we ourselves made in the past. So long as the war continues in Vietnam, of course, there is little possibility of any significant relaxation in our relations with China. But the Vietnam War is good reason for us to hurry in shifting our stance on the matter. Just because of the size of our military effort in Vietnam, our action would be less likely to be misunderstood as going "soft" on Communism or as a withdrawal of our commitments to our allies. Thus the war makes it easier rather than harder for us to shift stance on China. It also makes it more imperative.

We are drifting perilously close to war with China over Vietnam. Nothing would be more profitless or idiotic for both China and the United States than war. Neither side could possibly win such a war, but each could seriously hurt the other. We could not occupy China and force her to surrender, but we could destroy her cities and industries from the air. China could not hit us in any vital place, but it could bleed our manpower, and the war could ruin our relations with our important allies and with the Soviet Union. In fact, it might lead to a Soviet-American war that could destroy the world.

There is certainly no inevitability of a war between us and China. We live in such different political and economic environments that, like land and sea animals, we hardly meet. We have no reason to tangle with each other. If war does come, it will probably be because the Chinese seriously misunderstand our intentions. Their misconceptions of us are based in part on the fact that we have been unwilling to state what we really think about China and its future. We should at least clear away the falsities of our stance in the hope that this might diminish, even if only a little, the possibility of such a senseless war.

Another objection to a change in our stance on China is that it would not produce any quick *détente* with Peking. This is quite true. Peking would no doubt react with anger and scorn. Let us not forget, however, that China is an unstable country. The recent Red Guards fracas has once again shown this. Frustrations over repeated failures run deep. The leaders have become divided in their search for the road to progress. No one can predict what will happen in Peking, but it seems likely that within the next few years the Chinese will seek new approaches to their problems. Among these new approaches could be some amelioration in the Chinese attitude toward us, once the Vietnam War is over. We should make this more possible by removing the unnecessary insult implicit in our past posture on China and clarifying where we actually do stand. The sooner we do this, the more chance that it will have a beneficial effect on our relations with China.

Another objection to a redefinition of our China policy is that any sudden shift on our part would be upsetting to our small allies around China's rim, particularly at this time of tension in Southeast Asia, and would be regarded by the Chinese themselves as patent trickery. Both points have some validity. The United States, as I have said, is a great ship of state that can alter course only slowly. It would take many months of carefully planned statements to move us safely from our present unsound position to firmer terrain on which to stand in our relationship with China.

6. *The Future of Taiwan*

The most troublesome objection to changing our stance on China concerns Taiwan. If we were to redefine our attitudes, what would happen to Taiwan? If denied our recognition as the only rightful Chinese government, would Chiang's regime decide to capitulate to Peking? This should be recognized as a possibility, but it seems unlikely. Chinese have never been prone to suicide. In any case, Taiwan's demise as an independent state would do us no serious damage. We cannot afford to have the future of our relationship with 700 million Chinese determined for us by the leader of a small country of 13 million people.

I feel quite confident that if we redefine our China stance slowly and judiciously, Chiang's government will adjust to our new posture, even though it would maintain its claim to be the only China. While he and a small coterie of older men around him may still dream of reconquering the continent, the bulk of the people have no such ambition. Some 85 per cent are native Taiwanese—people whose ancestors came during the past few centuries from the coastal areas of South China and who speak the languages of that area. During their half century of rule by Japan, they diverged somewhat in attitudes and way of life from other Chinese, and almost to a man they hope for a Taiwan independent from Communist control and eventually run by the Taiwanese themselves. The younger elements among the mainland Chinese, who flocked into Taiwan at the time of the Communist triumph in China, are also coming to identify themselves with Taiwan. While intermarriage is still rare between them and the native Taiwanese, a common educational system that operates in standard North Chinese and a common way of life is gradually merging the two groups. Neither group wants to be subjected to Peking's harsh rule or absorbed into the poverty of the mainland.

Taiwan has in fact become a tremendous economic success in both light industries and agriculture. Starting with the foundation in modernization it acquired under Japanese colonial rule—scientific agriculture, a good railway system, good medicine, widespread education, and the like—and stimulated by a huge influx of human talent from continental China and economic aid from us, Taiwan has moved ahead with remarkable speed. In many ways it has come to rank in Asia next to Japan in levels of modernization. It has carried through a land-reform program second in thoroughness only to that of Japan. It has also come to play a significant role in technological aid to other rice-growing areas in the less developed world.

Politically Taiwan is less sound. Chiang Kai-shek, maintaining that Taiwan is only one of the smaller provinces that he rules, allows only a token representation of native Taiwanese in the central government and in the higher ranks of the army. While Taiwanese monopolize virtually all the elective posts in the provincial and local governments, they deeply resent this political and military domination by the mainlanders. They also remember the corrupt rule and the brutal political suppression carried out by Chiang's first representative in Taiwan after the Japanese surrender. The mainland leadership, in turn, is fearful of eventual engulfment by the native Taiwanese. For these reasons, there is uncertainty about what might happen when we withdraw, as we eventually must, our recognition of the Republic of China as the government of all China and still more uncertainty about what will happen when death or incapacity brings Chiang's dictatorial rule to an end. These may prove to be dangerous periods for Taiwan, but I believe that it will survive as a successful political and economic unit and that in time it will develop a democratic form of government. It already has elements of democracy at the local level and possesses the educational and economic underpinnings for full democracy.

Our attitude toward Taiwan, I feel, should be one of firm support for its right to self-determination and to membership in the United Nations. Its population of 13 million places it in the top third of the nations of the world in size. As a fundamental matter of principle, we can do nothing other than support its right to self-determination. Our defense of it from aggression across the Taiwan Straits should be part of this stance. Fortunately, its geographic position as an island and its comparatively stable society make its defense a relatively simple matter.

We should not, however, get involved in the problem of whether a separate Taiwan means that there are "two Chinas" or "one China and one Taiwan." Both Peking and Taipei fulminate against the so-called "two Chinas" plot, and "one China and one Taiwan" seems even worse to them. We, I feel, should be indifferent to the theory of the situation. This is a problem for Chinese, with their peculiar sensitivity to political division, to decide for themselves. All we need recognize is that two political entities do exist where only one had been before. Both should be in the United Nations. This is what is known as the "successor state" formula. We should allow the U.N. to decide which gets the Security Council seat, if either. China has not turned out to be one of the great stabilizing forces of the world, as had been expected in 1945. Perhaps the problem of the Security Council seat could be settled as part of a bigger reorganization, designed to bring the Council more in line with world realities.[1]

We should remember, of course, that, given the strong Chinese feeling about political unity, Peking will continue to regard our support of Taiwan's independence as the major barrier to a *détente* with us. They have made this clear all along. I suspect, however, that in time Peking will accommodate itself to the reality of an independent Taiwan, even if it does not accept it in theory. Chinese historically have shown greater capacities than most people for letting reality and theory follow separate courses.

We could contribute to Peking's accommodation by helping to eliminate those irritants that can be removed. Two of these are the island groups of Quemoy and Matsu, lying just off the Chinese mainland but occupied by Chiang's

[1] Just as an illustration of a more rational scheme than the present one, I might put forward the following. The nine countries that rank among the top twelve both in population and GNP might be given permanent seats. These are in the order they appear on the GNP list: the United States, the Soviet Union, West Germany, Japan, France, the United Kingdom, China, Italy, and India. Three—Pakistan, Indonesia, and Brazil—make only the population list as Nos. 5, 6, and 8; three others—Canada, Poland, and Australia—only the GNP list as Nos. 9, 11, and 12. These six, together with Mexico, which comes close to making both lists, might be put in a special category of frequently repeating temporary members. The other temporary seats could then be assigned to geographic groups of the other nations for occupancy in turn. The resultant body would come much closer to representing the world as a whole than does the present Security Council. This is not meant as a practical suggestion, since two of the countries, China and West Germany, are not even U.N. members, but it gives an indication of what a Council based on present world realities might look like.

forces. These symbolize to both sides the unfinished civil war. The Communists shell Quemoy ritually on alternate days in order to show their resolve to conquer Taiwan. Chiang holds on to the islands adamantly as symbols of his claim to the mainland. They actually weaken Taiwan's defense rather than strengthen it, because relatively large forces are tied down on these small islands, which could easily be by-passed in any attack on Taiwan. They also account for a good bit of Taiwan's disproportionately large expenditures for its military establishment. The islands thus serve only as an irritant to the Communists and a smoldering fire that might rekindle a broader conflagration. They are a drain on Taiwan and a menace to our interests. We should do our best to have these stumbling blocks to stability and "reconciliation" removed.

7. China's Place in the World

An even more serious barrier to a *détente* with China is our military posture in East Asia, which Peking views as military encirclement and preparations for its destruction. The Chinese Communists, I believe, are genuinely afraid of us. This accounts in part for their never-ending bluster about America being only a "paper tiger." Our professions that we want to live at peace and in cooperation with them will sound hollow as long as they feel that we are trying to draw a military noose around their necks.

We face a difficult problem in trying to strike an appropriate balance between adequate preparations to contain any Chinese attempt at open aggression and relaxation of our encirclement so that the Chinese might become less hostile and less aggressively inclined. We should, I believe, continue our defense posture in Japan, Okinawa, and Taiwan, and, as discussed below, in South Korea also. In Southeast Asia, however, we may in time find it possible to withdraw our military might a little farther from China's borders and to rely more on international guarantees for the security of this area. We shall consider this problem more fully in the next section. But here we should note that the smaller we can safely keep our defense establishment in East Asia and the farther we can keep it from China's borders, the better are the chances that China will accommodate itself to living peacefully with the rest of us.

I have suggested that China, as an unstable, troubled country, may try some shift in direction in the not too distant future. It could move toward a *détente* with us, if we help prepare the ground for this, but it is more likely that it will try other steps first before considering this. For example, an effort to unfreeze relations with the Soviet Union would make sense for the Chinese, though this might be too large and bitter a pill for the Chinese psychologically. A further rapprochement with some of our allies may be more probable. The fact that China's trade is largely with our allies is already a sign of this. Foreign trade is China's most important window on the world. It is in our long-range interest that this window should be as wide as possible, because through it China may learn enough about world realities to realize that it must adjust itself to them. A *détente* with our allies could well be a first step toward a *détente* with us and the reemergence of China into the world as a perhaps still troubled, but no longer seriously troublesome, member of international society.

In this regard, China's relations with Japan may prove particularly significant. As we have seen, Japan is already China's largest trading partner and chief foreign contact in other ways as well. The $621 million in trade between them in 1966 accounted for 15 per cent of China's total foreign trade. Peking also shows a sensitivity to Japan that it does not evince toward the other major industrialized nations. It notices Japanese criticism or bafflement at Chinese actions and tries to respond by explanations or corrections. By contrast, the Chinese seem merely hostile to reactions to their conduct in the United States or the Soviet Union and indifferent to reactions in Western Europe. The difference in their attitude toward Japan may be because of cultural and geographic closeness and because of shared literary idioms and close parallels in vocabulary (words of Chinese origin are used in Japanese, as we use words of Latin or Greek origin in English), which make understanding a little easier.

Another factor may be Peking's greater interest in trying to influence or dominate Japan as a neighbor whose industrial capacity would greatly enhance China's power, if harnessed to Chinese ambitions. There seems little doubt that at least some of the profits of Sino-Japanese trade and some of the cultural contacts between the two have been utilized by the Chinese to support political movements within Japan that were felt to serve Peking's interests.

This Chinese attempt to exert political influence on Japan has made some people fear that a rapid upsurge in trade and other relations between China and Japan could have an adverse political effect on Japan. There was considerable nervousness about this in both Japan and the United States during the 1950's, when Japan's economic future seemed less secure, the political situation in Japan was less stable, and the balance of economic power between China and Japan was less unfavorable to China than it is today. Even during this period, however, when Peking in 1958 tried to use the sudden stoppage of trade with Japan as a political weapon, the strategy backfired. Today fears that increased contact with China would have an adverse political effect on Japan are quite unrealistic. The exchange in goods between them that figures as 15 per cent of China's trade is a mere 3.5 per cent of Japan's trade. Japan is far the more stable of the two politically. If important political influences accompany trade and other contacts, these will almost certainly flow from Japan to China rather than in the other direction.

It could well be that Japan's most important bridge-building service to the world will be to help construct a bridge between the Chinese and the rest of us. Through Japan the Chinese may be best able to understand the realities of the outside world and may learn to adjust more realistically and more constructively to them. In any case, we should not be defensively nervous about relations between Japan and China but sympathetic and hopeful.

While I feel that we have tended to exaggerate China's threat to us and to world peace, we should not overcompensate for this by underestimating the problem China presents the world. China may be, in relative terms, a shrinking power in the world. It has nothing to gain from open aggression and finds its capacity to stir up revolutions in other ways dwindling. It will in time realize that it must take a less intransigent attitude toward the rest of the world. But China's gigantism will remain a problem for Chinese and for the world. A disturbed China is a great threat to world stability just because of its fantastic size. In the long run the chief problem it presents may not be the danger that it will be so rich and strong, as well as hostile, that it menaces our basic interests but rather that it may fall so far short of meeting the economic needs and aspirations of its people that it remains an unstable and sick fifth of humanity. A stable, contented, and reasonably prosperous China would constitute a great improvement in the world environment for all countries.

III

The Rest of Asia

I<small>T MAY</small> seem somewhat cavalier to assign Japan and China each a third of our interests in Asia and leave only the remaining third for all the other countries from Korea to Pakistan, but this is necessary if we are to achieve the sense of proportion we are seeking. Actually the "rest of Asia" is probably the smallest third in terms of our interests. It is roughly equal to Japan in total economic production but, because of the weight of its great population, much weaker in effective economic strength. Its population exceeds that of China by 10 or 20 per cent but, because of multiple divisions, has less real power in aggregate.

Our treatment of the rest of Asia in this section can be somewhat briefer than the treatment of Japan or China. Chapter Two was devoted primarily to this area and Chapter One to Vietnam. We need only pick up here the themes developed in these two chapters and add some practical conclusions regarding American foreign policy toward the area.

1. The Prospects for Asia

We have seen that China is not as great a menace to the rest of Asia as has been commonly assumed and that

Japan holds out more hope for the future of Asia than has generally been realized. Conditions within the rest of Asia, too, are cause, I feel, for confidence about the long-range future. The newer nations of Asia seem to have survived their birthpangs—the difficult transition from colonialism to independence. Most are slowly solidifying as nations and are making at least some economic and institutional progress. In some, economic growth is disappointingly slow—only marginally above population growth, if that—but even in these cases, foundations are being laid for future growth. There is, for example, the firming up of national consciousness and, most important of all, the spread of literacy and various other types of fundamental knowledge and skills. Thus, almost all the countries of the rest of Asia are becoming more viable as national units and, by the same token, less susceptible to domination from abroad.

One particularly hopeful sign in the past few years has been a great increase in the sense of regional solidarity, especially in Southeast Asia. The broad concept of Afro-Asian solidarity, which was so much talked about a few years back, has proved to be rather hollow. Across this vast area the peoples of the various regions know very little about one another and usually care less. Cultural differences separate them even more from one another than from the West, with which they often have more in common. All that unites them is their resentment of the West, but this negative force has little real binding power, as was indicated by the complete break-up at Algiers in June 1965 of the much-trumpeted Afro-Asian Summit Conference. However, smaller regional groupings of countries that are geographically close together and have more obvious common interests could prove quite significant.

During the past two years, in particular, there has been a veritable rash of negotiations and conferences, designed to establish useful regional ties. Some, such as the Association of South-East Asia (ASA), formed in 1961 by Thailand, Malaysia, and the Philippines, embrace only a small part of the region. Others, such as the Ministerial Conference for Economic Development, called together by the Japanese in the spring of 1966, and the Asian and Pacific Council (ASPAC), first convened by the Koreans the same year, cover a broader area. Some, like the Asian Development Bank, also formed in 1966, include the Indian subcontinent and even Afghanistan and Iran. In some of these organizations, Australia and New Zealand participate as regional countries. The presence of these advanced nations, like that of Japan, lends helpful solidarity to these efforts.

Regionalism in Asia is not likely to produce political mergers or even an economic community in the sense of the European Economic Community. Nationalism runs too deep for the first, and the economies of the countries of East and South Asia do not lend themselves to the second. There can be useful agreements on sharing certain costly technical or economic facilities. Schemes for regional economic development, such as for the Mekong River Valley in Laos, Thailand, Cambodia, and South Vietnam, may make sense. But on the whole, the economic relations of less developed countries are not basically with one another, but with the advanced nations. They provide the latter with raw materials and obtain from them complicated manufactured goods. Trade among the less developed countries is too much like taking in one another's laundry to be very significant. Japan, even if joined by Australia and New Zealand, is not big enough to play the balancing role of the industrialized sector for this vast underdeveloped area. Thus no very close political or economic groupings are likely to evolve in the foreseeable future.

Despite these limitations, however, regionalism, I believe, holds out great hope for Asia. It may help to overcome the frictions produced by ardent nationalism. By increasing interest in one another, it also adds, in a sense, to the strength and security of each country, because aggression against any one of them or even blatant attempts at subversion from abroad would arouse the concern of all and thus would be made politically, if not militarily, more costly.

In being so hopeful about the future of Asia, I open myself, I realize, to the charge of being too optimistic. It is somehow considered to be more "scholarly" to be pessimistic. The uninformed public is expected to live in a fool's paradise, but scholars are supposed to view things with alarm. An overly optimistic estimate is almost enough to blackball a scholar from acceptance by his fellows; mistakenly pessimistic estimates, no matter how numerous or how wrong, are forgiven or forgotten. In my own experience, however, I have noticed that though I have sometimes been forced to modify optimistic estimates for which I have been criticized, usually it has been to make them even more hopeful than before.

But let me qualify my optimistic tone. I am encouraged by the long-term trends in Asia because all along I have assumed that economic and institutional development would be a slow, painful process, that democracy would prove not fully feasible in much of Asia at present levels of development, and that there would be political instability for a long time. Given these assumptions, we can take heart at the progress Asia has made. It is laying the foundations for future more rapid growth—and in some areas, notably Taiwan, Malaysia, Thailand, and South Korea, the more rapid growth has already started. Genuine nations are beginning to take shape throughout Asia. There now seems little danger that a unitary Communist wave could sweep over the area. There is not even much danger that many, if any, countries will fall under the permanent control of outsiders of any sort.

We should note, however, some of the problems that still beset the countries of Asia—problems usually far greater than Japan or most of the countries of the West faced in their modernization process. The less developed countries of Asia find themselves discouragingly far behind the industrialized nations in economic progress. They feel that the terms of trade are running against them, as the prices for some of the raw materials they produce sag and prices for the manufactured goods they must import go on rising. They face, as we have seen, many cultural inhibitions to economic growth, and there are religious ones in addition, such as the Hindu unwillingness to slaughter the cows of India, which consume a great deal of food but give very little back to the economy.

Religion may also prove to be a bar in some places to the spread of birth control, which will be necessary if production is ever to move substantially ahead of population growth. In most Asian lands, ignorance and social tradition already are such large hurdles in the way of family planning that no one can be certain what other hurdles there may be. Only one thing is sure. Unless they bring their population growth under better control, few of the countries of Asia will make much progress toward even modest prosperity, and some, such as India, Pakistan, Ceylon, Indonesia, Taiwan, and Korea, may face a dismal future.

Despite their nationalistic enthusiasm, most of the countries of Asia still face serious problems of national solidarity. Three of the four lands in the world which were divided in the aftermath of the Second World War are in Asia—Korea, Vietnam, and China-Taiwan. Each, in part as a result of division, carries a crushingly heavy burden of military expenses. In addition, Taiwan has its division between native Taiwanese and mainlanders and Vietnam its Montagnard and Cambodian minorities and multiple religious divisions.

The Philippines have so many different languages that Tagalog, supposedly the national language, has not won out fully over them or English. In this predominantly Catholic land, there are also some very distinct religious and ethnic minorities, such as the Moslem Moros of Mindanao and several primitive pagan groups in Luzon and elsewhere.

Laos, despite its tiny population, is a welter of different ethnic groups. Singapore has a Chinese majority and Malay and Indian minorities, and Malaysia balances precariously between Malay Moslems, constituting not quite half of the total, Chinese, who are only slightly less numerous, and somewhat smaller communities of Indian Hindus and, in Borneo, Dayaks and other groups. Indonesia has a great deal of linguistic and cultural diversity over its broad expanse and an entirely separate Negroid society in West Irian (New Guinea), which Indonesians insisted on incorporating into their new nation only because it had for long appeared on maps as part of the Dutch East Indies.

In Burma the Burmans are all but surrounded by a variety of minority peoples, some of whom are battling for autonomy or even independence. The two widely separated sections of Pakistan differ sharply in language, climate, agriculture, and way of life, being united only by the Moslem religion. Nepal is divided between Indo-European Hindus and Mongoloid Buddhists. Ceylon has a Singhalese-speaking Buddhist majority, a very large Tamil-speaking Hindu minority, and a series of smaller ethnic groups. India has 14 official languages and scores of minor ones, scatterings of unassimilated "tribal" people, a remaining Moslem minority in a basically Hindu country, and a fantastically complicated social division by castes. All these problems make the troublesome French-Flemish division of Belgium and the French-English division of Canada or even the problem of racial minorities in the United States seem rather simple by comparison.

Because of these difficulties and the relatively low levels of technical skills that Asians can bring to bear on them, we must assume that there will be continuing political instability. We must remember that the chief problem of less developed countries is precisely that they are less developed. Many desirable techniques and policies that could be adopted by advanced nations are simply beyond their competence. One should not be surprised that so few of them are truly functioning democracies but rather that so many have managed to keep democratic institutions going as well as they have and that some are making progress in that direction. It should be noted that Korea, which not long ago was an almost complete military dictatorship, has made heartening progress toward democracy, and, as we have seen, considerable democracy has developed at the grass-roots level in Taiwan.

Still, coups and revolutions will, no doubt, continue to occur in many parts of Asia. In fact, domestic instability may become worse as the countries of Asia make further economic progress. The case of Japan has shown that the early stages of economic and institutional modernization can produce serious imbalances and strains in society. There is every reason to believe that Asia will continue to be a decidedly unstable part of the world.

Even taking all these problems into consideration, however, I believe that the long-range prognosis for Asia is reasonably good—that is, if we and the world can get past the hazards of the present situation in Vietnam. If we can really get *beyond Vietnam,* the basic situation within Asia seems to me promising and the world environment favorable. The capacities of the advanced countries for supplying technological and economic aid and their skills at providing it are increasing. World stability is growing, giving promise that the instabilities of Asia can be kept localized.

2. *Our Defense Role*

Even with this hopeful long-range estimate, there remains a short-range problem of security and defense in Asia. The overwhelming bulk of American wealth and manpower that has gone into Asia since the Second World War has been devoted to this problem. As we have seen, however, defense against open aggression across national boundaries no longer appears to be as big a problem as it once did. In part this may be simply because the past decade has given us a clearer idea of the realities of Asia. In part, it may be because the determined stand we took in Korea and elsewhere and the subsequent *détente* in relations between the Soviet Union and us has helped change the political climate of the world.

We have also come to see that the chief menace to the stability of most of the countries of Asia arises from conditions within them and that our own military power is relatively ineffective in meeting this problem. Our military strength becomes seriously watered down in guerrilla wars and, when deployed in battle in less developed countries, tends to build up political and economic countercurrents that nullify much of its force. Its use can get us all too easily into conflict with local nationalism or into a hopeless defense of an outmoded status quo. Nor is it necessarily in our long-range interests to try to preserve all regimes threatened by internal overthrow. Some countries need the reinvigoration of new governments and can achieve this in no way except revolution. Moreover, if we are not directly involved in combating such revolutions, we have more chance of establishing constructive relations with the new governments that follow them and of influencing these new governments to move in desirable directions.

Under these circumstances, I would like to suggest a simple rule of thumb to guide our policies in Asia: Any regime that is not strong enough to defend itself against its internal enemies probably could not be defended by us either and may not be worth defending anyway. In other words, if an Asian government, even with our technological and economic aid, is not able to defend itself against revolution or subversion, it is probably not a regime that we could prop up by a reasonable injection of our direct military power and very possibly is not one that in the long run is worth trying to maintain in any case. Such a rule of thumb would have kept us out of military involvement in Vietnam but not out of the Korean War. South Korea had proved well able to defend itself against internal subversion. Its problem was open and massive invasion from the North.

There can be little doubt that in the present state of world tension and great instability in Asia there is a desirable and necessary defense role for us to play in Asia, but we must learn how to fill this role without becoming committed to unnecessary and dangerous military involvements in civil wars. I would suggest that we should maintain substantial military power in the Western Pacific in order to deter aggression by keeping open a convincing option of the use of our military power to stop it. In particular we should hold the nuclear umbrella of our vast retaliatory power over any country threatened by Chinese nuclear blackmail. Even though the bulk of our aid should be of an economic and technical nature, I do not see why we should rule out the possibility of providing military and constabulary aid to regimes that seem more promising for the long-range development of their countries than what might supplant them. On the other hand, we should seek to minimize, if not entirely eliminate, our military presence in the less developed countries of Asia, and we should minimize alliances that commit us irrevocably to their defense, particularly in unilateral action, or run the risk of embroiling us in their civil wars.

It will not always be easy to draw the line between undesirable military roles and useful ones. I do feel, however, that we could keep our military power out of the less developed countries without too much difficulty. The core of our military strength in the Western Pacific is the Seventh Fleet, the greatest naval force in the world. It is based at sea, with support facilities largely at Yokosuka in Japan and back in Hawaii and on the West Coast. Subic Bay in the Philippines is its only important support facility in a less developed country, and it could probably be eliminated, if this seems desirable. Air power goes in part with the fleet and otherwise can be adequately maintained in Japan and Okinawa and on our own Western Pacific islands, such as Guam. Forward supplies can largely be stored in these same areas, and land forces are best held in reserve on our own soil.

Drawing a line between military aid and military involvement may be harder, but it can be done if we keep the distinction clearly in mind. Supplying materiel and training military personnel in the United States should offer no great problem. It might at times even be desirable to provide advisory military personnel to some Asian countries. However, this should be done with great care (as was not the case in Vietnam), and a sharp line should be drawn beyond this level of assistance—probably at the point of prohibiting our advisers from accompanying units into combat.

The involvement of other advanced countries would also help us from being drawn into civil wars in Asia. Even in the fields of economic and technological aid, the very fact that others are carrying a significant part of the burden would diminish the relative importance of our bilateral relationship with a less developed country and thus reduce the danger that our economic commitment would lead us to military overcommitment. In the case of constabulary or military aid, this would be even truer. Insofar as possible, these tasks in particular might best be undertaken by other advanced countries which, just because they are smaller and less powerful, are less likely than the United States to become embroiled in internal disturbances.

The crucial problem, however, would be the matter of formal defense commitments. We have in the past sought to align the less developed countries of Asia with us and to persuade them to enter into bilateral or multilateral defense treaties. This, I believe, was a mistake, and we should try to reverse our course. These treaties are dangerously binding to our freedom of action and have sometimes put our foreign policy in hostage to men like Syngman Rhee, Chiang Kai-shek, and Diem, who did not understand the principles for which we stand and, of course, did not have American interests at heart. The tail all too often seems to have wagged the dog.

Alliances with us also may give these less developed countries less security than if they took a more neutral posture between the major powers. They would do better to rely on their own unfettered nationalism, on regional groupings, on world opinion, and, if possible, on international guarantees, with our military power held in reserve for use only if necessary. American military power would still be there to stop aggression if it occurred, but, unencumbered by an alliance with us, each country could probably do better against the greater menace of internal subversion and would probably get broader worldwide support in case of either revolution or aggression. Neutralization, rather than alignment, seems to me both in their interests and in ours. In other words, in trying to foster stability in Asia, we should develop a policy that gives us greater flexibility, relies more on the indigenous strengths of the region, and encourages greater international participation.

Our course on alignments and alliances, however, is not one that can be quickly reversed. We can hold back from making new military commitments, and I would ardently hope that we do so, particularly in the case of large countries like India or Indonesia, because guerrilla wars in such countries would be far beyond our capacity to control. We cannot, however, repudiate the commitments we have already made, until something satisfactory to the Asian countries involved can take their place.

Japan, as a modernized nation, is, of course, a case apart that does not enter into the present discussion. I doubt very much, however, that we could or should in the foreseeable future remove our defense commitment from South Korea either. There is too much history behind it, and, in any case, South Korea is one of the firmest and therefore most defensible countries in Asia. Its sizable aid to us and South Vietnam in the present war, amounting at the present writing to about 40,000 fine fighting men, is a sign of this firmness and a token of our deep involvement with South Korea. I would hope, though, that in time our commitment itself would be enough to give South Korea security, and we could withdraw the two infantry divisions that are now stationed along the cease-fire line in Korea.

Taiwan also has its special history that will probably necessitate a continuing American defense commitment. Fortunately it too is a fairly solid unit, and it has a promising future if it can survive the two possible political crises we have discussed in the preceding section. Also it is an island, so defense is a relatively simple matter.

The Philippines, too, is an island country and we have a special historical involvement with it. Our commitment to defend it against external aggression will no doubt continue. Internal conditions, however, look less stable than those of South Korea or Taiwan. The economy is progressing more slowly, and the country is not able to feed itself, even though it is lush, tropical, and underpopulated. Corruption and petty lawlessness are rampant, and political morale is sagging. Administrative efficiency is declining, and the old Communist Huk insurgency is beginning to rise again. Under these conditions, American aid efforts evaporate into inefficiency and corruption and, as a consequence, have ground to a virtual halt.

Filipinos often assume that the United States will save them from their problems, no matter how serious these become. As a result, they tend to avoid facing up to these problems themselves, while blaming them on us. This results in a peculiarly virulent form of anti-Americanism. This is an unhealthy situation, and conditions are likely to continue to degenerate as long as it lasts. There is a need for a psychological disengagement of the United States from the Philippines. Only when the Filipinos realize that they must solve their own problems will they face them realistically, and only then can we be of much help to them. If this does not happen, the Philippines may have to go through some sort of political turmoil before it can begin to move ahead again. Under such circumstances, we should be on special guard against military involvement in internal instabilities.

Indonesia is another island country, and therefore our Seventh Fleet almost automatically provides it with a guarantee against aggression. However, it has not sought alignment with us; nor would it be wise for us to encourage this. Indonesia is a land of great potential importance. It is the sixth most populous country in the world, almost equaling all the rest of Southeast Asia combined, and it has considerable natural resources. But the serious economic decline that set in under Sukarno's irresponsible rule has still not been stopped. While the new government is approaching Indonesia's problems with vigor and realism, impatient popular expectations may not give it the time it needs to turn the situation around and get Indonesia back on the road to economic growth. Indonesia has long-range promise, but faces serious growing pains before the promise can be fulfilled.

Most of the countries of South Asia, too, have not sought alignment with us, and the alliance we have had with Pakistan through SEATO has become meaningless because of Pakistan's virtual withdrawal. Except for Ceylon, these countries are all continental, and this fact, together with their great distance from the United States and their huge populations, makes any American defense role very difficult. India and Pakistan are the second and fifth most populous countries in the world. It is true that they are doing better economically than Indonesia, even though they are less generously endowed by nature. Pakistan in particular, having shaken free from restrictive Marxian dogmas, is doing quite well. Still, no one could guarantee the internal stability of any of the countries of South Asia over the decades ahead. This too is an area where we should try to avoid firm military commitments or involvement in problems of internal stability.

The Southeast Asian mainland presents us with the greatest dangers and offers the greatest problems. No course can be charted for our relations with Vietnam and Laos until the fighting in these countries is brought under control, but we must strive in the long run to get ourselves out of military commitments to their domestic stability. In Thailand we are right now in the process of greatly increasing our military presence and therefore our commitments, but this too is an outgrowth of the Vietnam War. Most of our military forces in Thailand are there in support of our efforts in Vietnam, and much of the rest is involved in the insurgency that has recently started in the poor northeastern corner of the country and seems related, at least in part, to the war in Vietnam.

Some people fear that this insurgency is the beginning of a full-scale guerrilla war, as in Vietnam. China is playing a much larger and more direct role in stirring up the guerrilla activities in Thailand than it ever did in South Vietnam, and the presence of a Vietnamese refugee population complicates the situation even further. Moreover, our growing military forces in Thailand may so disrupt the economy and society as to increase internal instability and insecurity.

Thailand, however, is a decidedly more stable country than Vietnam. It has a long history of independence. It is true that Thailand is a military dictatorship, under a king, and that, outside of the capital district, the peasants, as elsewhere in Southeast Asia, think mostly in local terms and have little sense of the national unit. But Thailand on the whole is fairly prosperous and has been moving ahead economically. Only the neglected northeast and the extreme south, where there is a Malay minority, are disturbed. Thailand thus is not likely to fall apart in the way Vietnam did.

In any case, it would be very difficult for us to reduce our military presence and quite impossible to cut down on our military commitments to Thailand until the wars in Vietnam and Laos are over or at least greatly reduced in scale. We should, however, try to move in this direction when peace is restored to Southeast Asia. It would be better both for us and for the people on the mainland of Southeast Asia if that whole area were to be recognized as neutral in the frictions between us and the great Communist powers.

Of course, as I have said, our ability to reduce military commitments in Asia depends to a large extent on the development of satisfactory substitutes. Our attempt through SEATO to find an international answer to the problem of instability in Asia has proved a failure. French and British membership in SEATO is now almost meaningless, and in the Vietnam War even Australia and New Zealand have offered little more than token support. SEATO has shrunk to a unilateral American undertaking. This, together with our various bilateral defense treaties with Asian countries, makes the other powers look upon the stability of the region as an American problem. It is not. It is a world problem, and their interests are as much involved as ours.

One would hope that the U.N. might be the answer, but it gives little promise of this at present. Other types of international guarantees against aggression, however, may prove more feasible. Our overcommitment in Asia has perhaps inhibited the development of such broader guarantees. A more modest estimate of our interests and role in securing the stability of Asia might induce others to put a higher estimate on their own interests and roles. The Asian countries themselves and the advanced states of the West all have interests in stability in Asia. So also does the Soviet Union, since Asian instability is a threat to world peace and since

China, in the rivalry between it and the Soviet Union for leadership among the Communist nations, is more likely to gain from continued instability in Asia than are the Russians. A much broader international approach to the problem of Asian security would seem feasible to me, and if it were achieved it would give us much firmer international footing in the event that we were again forced to use military power to attempt to halt aggression.

3. Attitudes Toward Our Aid Role

If we could cut back on our military commitments in Asia, we probably would be able to play a larger role in giving economic and technological aid than we have in the past. This would be putting the weight of our effort where it would count most. As we have seen, economic and institutional development is far more important for the future of Asia than immediate defense.

It would not be merely a matter of shifting some of our own military savings to an increased aid program. The countries of Asia, too, should be persuaded to divert less of their meager resources to military preparation against each other. A sizable part of our own aid to them goes into the economically unproductive field of military weapons. I recognize the need of sometimes supplying Asian countries with military and constabulary aid against domestic insurgency, and there are some cases—notably South Korea, Taiwan, and India—in which weapons from us may be needed to help diminish the possibility of Communist aggression. I see little point, however, in our providing Asian countries with jets or tanks that can only be used against one another. We should not be persuaded by the argument that if we do not supply them the Russians or possibly the Chinese will. In the long run, this will prove as profitless to these others as it is to us. "Friendship" bought with weapons is not worth having.

India and Pakistan make a good case in point. Their armament against each other constitutes a tragic misuse of the resources of the area. I doubt that outsiders can force on them a settlement of the emotion-charged Kashmir issue —though it might be worth trying to do this. International guarantees, however, could be set up to give them security against each other as well as against the unlikely possibility of a Chinese attempt at conquest. The resultant reduction by India and Pakistan of investments in armies and weapons would perhaps be the greatest economic boon we could help bring to either country.

It has been popular for some time, in this country and elsewhere in the world, to castigate American ineptness in giving aid to other countries. Much of this criticism is quite unfair. No doubt, we have made mistakes of all sorts, but the giving of aid is no simple matter, and it takes time to learn how to do it well. As we have seen, the whole concept of aid was a major breakthrough in international relations that the United States pioneered in the early postwar years, and we should be proud of this and of the fact that the American people have been willing to support it year after year since then. We should recognize, however, that all too much of our aid effort has been wasted and some of it has even worked against our own interests. We must learn to do better.

We should first get a clearer understanding of what the role of our aid in Asia really is and what the problems we face in trying to make it effective really are. Aid to a temporarily stricken advanced nation is comparatively easy. It is short-term, and problems of national pride thus do not become deeply involved. Aid to the less developed countries of Asia, however, will go on for decades, and national sensitivities have already been rubbed raw by history.

We must first of all get away from thinking of our aid efforts in Asia as a crash program to build up the countries behind our military defense lines. This may have been appropriate at one time in Europe, but it is not applicable to Asia today. The crash-program mentality and the emphasis on military defense do little to strengthen Asian countries against their major danger of internal instability. At the same time, such efforts contribute relatively little to the long-term growth that is the important thing in Asia. Our aid should be aimed primarily at helping them in this long-range development.

I think we should also get away from the idea that aid is a tool for building alignments and winning friends. As we have seen, we should be cutting back on alignments in any case, and the long-range health of the Asian countries is of much more importance to us than their short-range friendship. The friendship of less developed countries, particularly if bought by aid, is not a great asset to anyone. We should turn a cold shoulder on Asian countries that try to control our aid or diplomatic policies by threats of abandoning their "friendship" for us.

We should not be worried about Soviet aid programs or feel ourselves in competition with them. The more real economic aid the Soviet Union gives to the less developed countries, the better for all of us. In any case, aid reveals two faces in a popularity contest. All people are proud, and a natural resentment builds up against those from whom one receives largess. We should look at aid in a calculating and dispassionate way as an investment in our future world environment, not as a stratagem in the present balance of power in the world, because there is very little balance of power actually involved, but the future of humanity is definitely at stake.

Most important, we must get away from thinking that our aid programs make us the leaders or guides of the countries of Asia. I presume that it is our long missionary tradition toward Asia that lets us slip so easily into this role. While one cannot but admire the fine spirit and substantial achievements of individual Americans motivated by missionary zeal, this is not a suitable role for us as a nation in the second half of the twentieth century. Asians do not want us as leaders or teachers. Their attitude should be thoroughly understandable, especially considering their recent colonial past. No people is willing to let another take leadership in its own affairs. We certainly did not let the Europeans chart our course across the American continent, though in that simpler day we were happy to use their capital and skills. We are acceptable in Asia as outside friends and helpers, but not as inside leaders.

The chief hope for healthy development in Asia is the nationalistic ardor of its various peoples, and the main outside influences that can help in this development are the wealth and skills of the United States and the other advanced nations. The problem is that these internal and external forces, instead of working together in harmony, can all too easily work against each other. We must learn how best to reduce friction between them and make them pull together.

Most fundamental to this problem is the matter of attitude. We must be crystal-clear in our own minds that we cannot be inside leaders but only sympathetic outside helpers. We must constantly remind ourselves that it is someone else's country we are dealing with, not ours. We must realize that each country has its own way of doing things and that ours may not be practical or desirable for other people. We should not be the sponsors of economic, social, or political development in Asian countries, but only supporters of Asians who are trying to achieve this development. We should not be trying to create better societies for them but should merely be helping them in their efforts to create the sort of societies they want, if these seem to us to be a step in the right direction. We cannot export democracy to others, only support them in their efforts to develop it. Whatever the original models may have been, Japanese democracy was made not in the United States or in England but in Japan. If democracy is to succeed elsewhere in Asia, it must be home-grown too.

We run serious and unwarranted risks when we take the initiative in sponsoring important internal changes in an Asian country or when our influence becomes so strong that we assume responsibility for the existence or nature of a regime. As in the military field, we are likely to stir up nationalistic countercurrents, and we run the danger of becoming responsible for internal stability, which we cannot really guarantee. Our aid is often of such importance to an Asian country that it seems to dominate it and its policies. This is not a healthy situation. It is almost certain to produce anti-Americanism or sycophancy, or probably a combination of the two. I do not advocate reducing our aid in such cases, but I do think we should attempt to reduce the external pressure aid can represent. We will probably be able to be of much greater help, and therefore of more real influence, if we do not seek to lead in Asia but simply to serve as outside supporters of individual or collective Asian initiative.

If this were to be our attitude toward our aid role, it would help us solve what has been one of our most puzzling dilemmas. We have constantly been bothered by the question of how much aid we should give to countries whose nature and actions we cannot approve. Can we rightly give aid to them if they are not democratic and do not seem to be progressing in that direction or if they fail to undertake badly needed reforms? Should we attach tight strings to our aid that will force them to do what we consider politically desirable?

Political strings, I think, should be avoided. The attempt to exercise leadership, even in this negative way, probably does more harm than good in the long run. I believe that, regardless of the situation in a country or the nature of its government, we should extend to it whatever aid we can, if, in our judgment, this aid will help it toward long-range growth and development. We should not provide aid that permits it to avoid taking desirable but painful steps it is capable of taking. In other words, we must not underwrite injustice, backwardness, or incompetence. On the other hand, many Asian countries are at present incapable of operating democratic forms of government or of taking many of the steps that we would consider desirable. In such cases, if our aid were to help lay the foundations for future healthy development, it would be in our interest and in theirs. In any case, however, we should attempt to avoid the sort of involvement in a regime and its policies that make us responsible for its existence or nature.

This last statement may sound as if I were objecting to our efforts to induce the South Vietnamese government to develop democratic institutions, carry through a desirable land-reform program, and take the various constructive economic and social measures in the countryside that are subsumed under the curious term of "pacification." I do not mean this at all. In a situation such as that in Vietnam, in which we have already become deeply committed to a regime and our own intervention is largely responsible for its continued existence, we are inevitably responsible for the nature of that regime too. We are committed to trying to make it as good as it is capable of becoming. Moreover, improvement of Saigon's political, economic, and social policies is an important factor in trying to bring the war to a close. As I have pointed out, however, the Vietnam War is exactly the sort of situation we should try to avoid. To do this, we should understand that we can neither guarantee the countries of Asia from internal instability nor provide them leadership in domestic reform.

Some people may find my attitude toward helping Asia too calculating, cold, and aloof, but I feel that our mistake often has been to become too emotionally involved and too intimate. I take this somewhat detached attitude toward Asians because I respect them and their differences from us. I should hope they would be similarly detached and respectful toward us. I particularly decry the tendency of many Westerners to cover up their essential disdain for Asian civilizations by trying to demonstrate an appreciation that they do not really feel. Japan has shown us that there is much to admire and a great deal for us to learn from the civilizations of Asia, but I get very uneasy when I see Americans who know little about Asian cultures professing to admire the "native" art, music, or customs. This is patronizing. It is a kind of arrogance.

I believe that we should, in general, be less eager to urge aid on Asian countries and more careful in giving it. If we played somewhat harder to get, our aid might be better used—and, incidentally, more appreciated. We must be clear in our own minds and make crystal-clear to others that economic growth and political and social reform in an Asian country are far more important to its inhabitants than to us. No country should think that it can get us over the barrel by threatening its economic or political suicide. Sometimes, however, our government officials, in their efforts to win Congressional support for aid programs, and our experts, in their eagerness to arouse public interest, "oversell" the importance of Asian countries to the United States. We should avoid this and also situations in which the acceptance of American aid becomes a way for an Asian government to avoid having to adopt difficult or unpleasant reforms. Our aid should go only to regimes that show a willingness to take the painful measures needed and to projects that support rather than inhibit necessary reforms.

I wish to emphasize, however, that I am not suggesting that we reduce the overall amount of our aid when I say that we should insist that it be used effectively. Actually the more successful we are in finding productive uses for our aid, the more scope there will be for the further efficient use of such funds. I believe that we should, in fact, greatly expand our aid efforts. This, I feel sure, we can do with no great difficulty. If we can end the war in Vietnam, reduce our military commitments, and put less emphasis on military aid, the resultant savings to the American taxpayer would far exceed any sum that could be used effectively for foreign aid.

4. *Organizing Our Aid Activities*

We face two specific problems in implementing our aid policies. We must devise means to keep our aid from committing us to a guarantee of the internal stability of a country or to the maintenance of its government or the status quo. We must also see to it that it does not become so dominating an influence in a country that it stirs up fierce resentments against us. One way to try to achieve both objectives would be to channel as much of our aid as is feasible through international agencies, such as the International Bank, the Asian Development Bank, ECAFE (Economic Commission for Asia and the Far East), and various international consortia. I doubt very much, however, that this will prove a solution to the whole problem. International agencies are likely to be even more tied down by redtape and bureaucratism than are national agencies. They lack flexibility and move ponderously. They suffer from even greater waste of resources in overhead. We should look with favor on the international approach to aid whenever possible, but, if we are to play the full role we should, we will probably have to continue large bilateral aid programs as well.

For these a useful approach to the problem might be to attempt to separate the providing of aid funds from the development of aid programs and their administration. The

United States, as a government, might play more the role of banker than of social worker. Our government would sit back and wait for Asian countries to come up with specific aid proposals. These, we would insist, should be well conceived, well organized, and practical. In other words, they should be neatly packaged and tied up with their own strings. This would avoid the problem of whether or not we ourselves should attach strings to our aid. We would simply decide whether a proposal was wise and feasible and included a convincing plan for successful implementation. If it met these criteria, we, as the banker, could then underwrite it financially, by grants or loans, assuming it fell within our financial ability.

The objection to such an approach might be that the most difficult parts of an aid program are planning and executing it, rather than finding the money to finance it, and that the less developed countries, because of their lack of adequate skills, are no more able to perform these functions by themselves than to finance the projects. This is quite true. But it remains psychologically and politically unsound for the American government to be performing either of these functions for Asian countries. We need other agencies for this, and these we should be able to devise with a little use of imagination.

Some existing international agencies may be able to fill part of the need. As a basic aid project also, substantial funds could be provided less developed countries to help them develop adequate planning agencies and administrative staffs for development projects, by hiring from all over the world the kind of experts needed. Special emphasis might be placed on obtaining experts from small countries rather than the big powers. These experts would assure the aid-providing country of the soundness of the aid proposals and the feasibility of their execution. At the same time, as employees of the aid-receiving country, they would be less abrasive to national sensitivities than employees of a foreign country would be. They also would probably be more valued. I am thinking of the experience of Japan in the nineteenth century, when it very effectively used foreign experts in these capacities. The only difference would be that, in contrast with the Japanese case, this expert help would be paid for by the aid-giving countries.

Another technique might be the use of more extra-governmental institutions. We boast of our free-enterprise system. Here is a good chance for us to show its advantages. I am not thinking merely of private investment. This is very important, but, because of Asian fears of "economic imperialism," it has certain limitations. I have more in mind the use of private foundations for cultural and educational activities and perhaps private nonprofit corporations for economic development. To perform fully the tasks of which they would be capable, such foundations and corporations might in most cases need government financing. Thus they would become in a sense semigovernmental agencies, but, if they were permitted to operate within broad guidelines under their own private boards of directors, they would help keep the government one step removed from planning for other sovereign states and operating programs within their boundaries. They would thus reduce the political and psychological hazards of the whole aid situation and, I feel sure, would operate much more efficiently and with less overhead than would direct governmental agencies. To the extent that they were free of minute government supervision, they could move with greater speed and more flexibility than could full government agencies, and they would stir up fewer countercurrents.

In any case, however aid is provided or administered, we have a deep interest in having it used as effectively as possible. We should be particularly on guard against our natural love for big and spectacular undertakings. This is all the more true because it coincides too closely with common Asian desires to achieve showy results for prestige purposes.

Asians sometimes want great steel plants, jet airlines, imposing public buildings, or magnificent highways before the local economy is really able to support these ostensible manifestations of progress.

We should insist on careful tip-to-tail studies of the costs of any major project. For example, a proposal for building a steel mill should take into consideration not only the costs of building and maintaining the necessary transportation facilities but also the costs of the educational institutions needed to provide it with the necessary flow of technicians. Not infrequently the grandiose scheme will prove economically much less advantageous than small-scale, grass-roots undertakings. In some areas and at certain stages of development, small home industries may be more valuable than large factories, or primary and secondary schools and their teachers may be more needed than large dams or broad highways.

Special emphasis should also be placed on increasing agricultural production, for most of the lands of Asia are still basically agricultural and considerable growth in agriculture is necessary for any very great economic advance. The other side of the coin is population control. This is, of course, a delicate field for foreign aid. It is unwise for international agencies or foreign private groups, to say nothing of the American government, to try to force family planning on any country. But wherever there is a local desire for populaton control, we should give it maximum support.

Parallel with aid problems are those of trade. In the long run the development of markets for the goods of the less developed countries is even more important for their healthy economic growth than is aid. Whenever possible the emphasis should be on trade rather than aid, because trade is self-sustaining, while aid is actually a temporary distortion of natural economic processes.

One of the most effective ways to give an economic

boost to the less developed countries would be to develop larger markets in the advanced nations, first for their agricultural and mining products and then for the products of their light industries. This could not be done without prejudice to some economic interests in the advanced countries, but it would be less costly to the economies of these countries as a whole than aid provided from taxes. It would also fit better into the long-range economic development of both the advanced and the less developed nations. The less developed countries will almost inevitably expand their role as providers to the advanced nations of primary products and light industrial goods, and as they do this, they will themselves become better markets for the more complicated products that the advanced countries are best at making. To the extent that this process can be speeded up, the less developed countries will advance economically at greater speed—and at less total cost and with more benefit to the advanced nations as well.

I do not profess to be an expert on aid matters, never having participated in either the formulation or the administration of aid programs. Those who know the field may see serious flaws in my suggestions. But, if so, I feel certain that they could propose other ways to meet the problems. As a nation, we have responded generously with dollars to the worldwide need for aid, but I do not think that we have devoted enough of our brainpower to it. We have not clearly analyzed what is needed and how we can best provide it. We have tended to subordinate aid to our sometimes mistaken concepts of the needs for defense, not realizing that aid in the long run is more important than defense. We have at times tried to play politics with aid—seeking through it to win friends or strengthen support for our views in the U.N. or in international controversies. We should see that our greatest interest in Asia is its development over the long term into a healthy, stable, and reasonably prosperous half of the world and that, since our capacities for giving economic and technological aid are our greatest asset for helping in this process, we should devote our brains and efforts toward finding ways to use this asset effectively.

5. *A Second Look at Vietnam*

After this quick glance over our relationship with Asia as a whole, we might look back again at Vietnam to try to see it in a little better perspective. If the area I have defined as "the rest of Asia" is, in terms of our interests, merely a third of the whole—and possibly the smallest third at that—and if South Vietnam is, in population and production, only about 2 per cent of this third, we can see all the more clearly how disproportionate to our interests has been our great investment of lives and wealth in this small corner of Asia. Looking at Vietnam in this light, we may be better able to judge what sort of settlement there would be consonant with our interests.

It should be clear that almost any settlement, short of China's domination of Vietnam, would be satisfactory to us, so long as it is consistent with the commitments we have made to the people of South Vietnam. No Vietnamese, North or South, wants Chinese domination, so that should present no great difficulties. It is not to our interests to maintain military bases in Vietnam over the long run or to try to keep South Vietnam aligned with us. We can afford to be very generous in permitting its neutralization and the establishment of international guarantees to take the place of our commitments. The only real problem is our commitments as they now stand. Briefly summarized, they are to give the people of South Vietnam a chance for peaceful self-determination and for this purpose to prevent domination by military force, whether this be by aggression or insurrection. These commitments were made to the Saigon government and those who accept its leadership, but we must remember that the Vietcong and their supporters constitute a sizable part of the South Vietnamese population and that all Vietnamese, Southerners as well as Northerners, hope that someday Vietnam will be a stable, united country.

As I have said, there seems little chance for a settlement until the scale of the war has been lessened and until the other side has come to realize that the United States is not going to back down and that they, therefore, have little prospect of victory. This situation might best be achieved by sealing off the South from the North by a barrier at the 17th parallel and into Laos, thus limiting the guerrilla war in the South to the recruits and weapons that can be found locally; by stopping the bombing of the North as soon as is feasible and certainly by the time such a barrier has been established; by a careful program of "pacification" of the South, starting with the retraining of the ARVN (Army of the Republic of Vietnam) so that it will be capable not only of local defense, but of political, economic, and social reconstruction and thus, through the meeting of grass-roots desires as well as through defense, will be able to win to Saigon the support of the peasantry and to deny the manpower and production of rural Vietnam to the Vietcong; and finally by maintaining, and if possible increasing, the military superiority we have already established in the South. This is not a quick strategy, but it may be the only one that can succeed.

For the crucial "pacification" phase to succeed, however, the ARVN and the peasants they are seeking to "pacify" must be given hopes for the future. There must be personal and national objectives, formulated not so much in American terms as in terms that are understandable to the local people and appeal to them. This is what Communists usually do—often in pie-in-the-sky form—but still in ways that are effective in winning them popular support.

There also must be reasonable alternatives to a continuation of the war for the Vietcong, or at least for the more moderate or war-weary elements among them. Generous but realistic proposals for a settlement made early could appreciably shorten the war by winning more support for Saigon, internally and internationally, and causing some Vietcong to waver in their determination. One element of such an approach to the problem should be thoroughgoing reform efforts in South Vietnam—in land reform, in local self-government, in basic human rights, and in many other areas. It should be made clear that Saigon is in the process of achieving the very things for which some Vietcong supporters feel they are fighting.

Another element, I feel, should be a realistic role for those Vietcong who are willing to attempt to reach a negotiated settlement. I do not think that this can be provided simply by a promise of a chance to vote in elections. The Vietcong are not believers in the democratic process, nor is South Vietnam at this stage the sort of country in which democracy is likely to operate fully and smoothly. The Vietcong will not stop fighting, I feel, until they have something more tangible than this. A share in the Saigon government (except insofar as this is won through elections) seems to me quite unrealistic. It would mean nothing to the Vietcong unless their representatives in the government were backed up by their own independent military power, in which case it would probably be only a steppingstone to their seizure of the whole government by force.

A more realistic approach, I feel, might be a cease-fire arrangement under which zones that at the time are really controlled by the Vietcong would remain in their hands, while steps were being taken, presumably under some sort of international supervision, to establish economic and administrative contacts between these zones and the rest of South Vietnam and to spread common reform measures and administrative systems throughout South Vietnam, thus slowly leading to its actual reunification. Such a settlement would, of course, leave many dangerous ambiguities, but it may be the only way to bring a relatively speedy end to the war. We continually hear of South Vietnamese villages that have been under firm Communist control for more than twenty years. To root the Communists out of every one of these villages may take years of fighting. It may in fact be quite impossible. Some risks may have to be run if we wish to bring this war to an end.

Still another element in a settlement, I believe, should be proposals for the eventual reunification of North and South Vietnam. At first this might be merely the creation, again under international supervision, of special organs to coordinate the economies of the two regions for their mutual benefit, but the ultimate aim would be a gradual reintegration of North and South as a single country. Despite the Southerners' traditional fear of Northern domination, unification is basically the dream of all Vietnamese, and it is a dream that should be encouraged and helped to fruition.

Naturally any settlement should include a fairly definite schedule for the removal of the American military establishment from South Vietnam. The other side would never settle for anything less, and it is in our long-range interests. An American military withdrawal, of course, would increase the risks that the settlement would not prove stable, but, in view of the dismal prospects for us and for Vietnam if there is no settlement, these chances would seem worth taking. If such an approach were to prove unworkable, it would probably fall apart long before we had withdrawn much of our military power or before the Vietcong had gained any great military advantage from the cease fire. In that case, the advantages to Saigon and to us in having made the effort might offset whatever disadvantages there were.

Another danger would be that the Saigon government might not prove adequately cooperative in such a program. But this too may be a risk worth taking. I have argued against our trying to take the leadership in other people's countries, but in Vietnam we have already assumed this undesirable role. We need now to show leadership in finding ways to get us out of this role for the future. In any case, if the Saigon government were to sabotage efforts to find a reasonable compromise peace, this, together with the international supervision that would probably be part of any effort at such a compromise settlement, might serve to relieve us of the commitments we have made in Vietnam without the disastrous consequences I outlined in Chapter One.

It could be argued that none of the above proposals are realistic because the Vietcong would never accept anything short of complete victory. This is probably true of the Communist leaders and cadres. They would accept a cease fire only out of dire necessity and with the intention of resuming their attempt to seize power by military force as soon as possible. Their rank-and-file peasant supporters, however, are different. If they found a settlement met many of their wishes, they might no longer be responsive to orders from the Vietcong leaders. The middle ground would have shifted to Saigon's side. This is the chief advantage of a cease fire, because it would permit us to begin to use our great economic power effectively to tip the scales of popular support in Saigon's favor. It is for this reason that a cease fire—even of the dubious sort I have described above—may be a chance well worth taking.

In these suggestions, I am not trying to outline a specific plan for ending the Vietnam War and getting us out of this situation that is so adverse to our long-range interests. I am merely trying to illustrate the flexibility we should show in trying to find a solution. If we were to devote to this problem even a small measure of the imagination and energy we have devoted to prosecuting the war in Vietnam, we might much better serve our own interests and those of the Vietnamese people.

Chapter Four

Postscript: Preparing for Our Role in Asia

I HAVE called this final brief chapter a postscript because it is not about our immediate relationship with Asia or the direction in which we should try to guide it. Rather, it concerns the longer-range need to prepare ourselves better to meet the great challenges posed by Asia and the rest of the less developed world. I have in mind two major problems: the inadequacy of our instruments for planning and conducting our foreign relations as a whole, and the still greater inadequacy of the knowledge and understanding we as a people bring to our foreign relations, especially those with Asia.

Neither of these shortcomings is surprising. We have moved very rapidly—within a few decades—from a position of relative isolation and a minor role in world affairs to deep involvement and heavy responsibilities as the strongest nation in what is now a much more closely interrelated world. Only a half century ago our national well-being seemed to be little affected by what happened abroad, particularly in the less developed regions, which in large part were inside the empires of other countries. There seemed little reason to put much emphasis on foreign relations or on learning about distant lands. Today, however, what happens abroad presents us with our most serious challenges—not only because a nuclear exchange or even less drastic forms of war could imperil our national existence, but also because we bring much less knowledge to bear on our foreign relations than we do on our domestic problems.

Actually we have responded reasonably well to this change in priorities in our problems. I doubt that any other major country has done as much to restructure its foreign relations and the agencies that conduct them. With the possible exception of the Soviet Union, none has made anything like our effort to develop expert knowledge about the rest of the world, and certainly none has done as much in popular education. In comparison with the other countries of the West or Japan, we have no reason to be embarrassed. But what we have done is still far from adequate, simply because our size makes our role and our responsibility so much larger than theirs.

1. *Formulating Foreign Policy*

There is a general realization of the inadequacy of our agencies for formulating and conducting our foreign relations. Much of the criticism is focused on the State Department, which is accused of being a "bowl of jelly" or, in older imagery, a haven for effete "cookie pushers." Neither charge is at all fair. From my own personal experience, I know that the Foreign Service is made up for the most part of able and extraordinarily hard-working and dedicated people. Foreign Service Officers, I believe, work harder than do corresponding members of the rest of the government bureaucracy or the officer corps of the military. Their wives perform extensive and important volunteer service for their country. If the State Department as a whole fails to fulfill its functions adequately as the chief formulator and executor of foreign policy—and I am afraid that the charge is correct—the blame should be placed not so much on it and its personnel as on the American government and people for failing to give enough attention to foreign policy and to develop adequate organs for its prosecution.

As our foreign relations have increased rapidly in size and complexity, we have allowed responsibility for them to scatter throughout the federal government. Coordination and a sense of proportion have both suffered. Piecemeal reactions take the place of carefully thought-out long-range policies. The State Department, which is held responsible for giving shape and cohesion to our foreign policies, has not been given adequate authority, and, in any case, it and the Foreign Service have been starved of the talent and funds that would be needed to do the job properly.

Because of the tremendous strength of our country and the resultant vast size and complexity of its foreign relations, we face a very difficult problem in trying to formulate balanced and farsighted policies and keep our manifold activities abroad properly coordinated. Our government is both huge and complex, and the interaction between its various parts is extremely complicated. No single part of the government, such as the State Department, can fully control or even coordinate the formulation and execution of foreign policy. This can be done only at the very top of the whole government structure. But the President, his immediate aides, and the top officers in the State Department and in the other parts of the federal government are all so incredibly busy handling an infinite number of immediate problems that they are never really able to study and think through thoroughly the complexities of all our long-range problems and their bearing on one another. The men at the top must jump from crisis to crisis, thus staying behind our problems as they develop rather than ahead of them. Policies are commonly produced by specific responses of a variety of governmental agencies to specific problems as they arise. All too often the response is determined by the branch of government most immediately involved—say the military or one of its three arms—and more important national interests represented by other branches of the government may not be taken into consideration. Sometimes the possible alternatives to the response chosen or its long-range implications are not considered at all.

At a simpler and slower-moving period in history this traditional way of meeting problems as they arose was perhaps adequate. We, the British, and many other peoples have "muddled through" in this manner for a long time. But the inadequacy of this approach has been shown all too clearly in Vietnam. For lack of deep enough thought soon enough about the problem as a whole, we now find ourselves superbly equipped and organized and performing at a high level of technical competence, but engaged in an operation that should never have been undertaken. Obviously we need to devise better policy-formulating mechanisms. We also need to devote more of our national talents and resources to the study and formulation of foreign policy, particularly with regard to areas such as Asia about which our knowledge is relatively thin.

The businessman no longer just responds to problems as they arise. He tries to foresee changes in demand or shortages of supply before they arise and plans in advance how to deal with these problems or avoid them. We build roads not just in response to traffic jams as they occur but in anticipation of what the traffic will grow to be. The development of military airplanes, ships, and weapons is scheduled far in advance and on the basis of estimates regarding all sorts of future developments. It is folly to let foreign policy, the most important field of all, limp along in nineteenth-century style, responding to problems as they arise.

One gets the impression that the Pentagon puts careful effort into the study of the weapons we might use to carry through a military policy, but that the State Department and the whole government structure devote much less attention to trying to determine how to avoid the need to use these weapons or how to use them to best advantage to further American interests, if this proves necessary. Individual American corporations seem to put more effort and thought into their specific interests in our foreign economic contacts than the government puts into the overall shaping of the general framework in which these individual actions take place. Broad decisions that may affect the whole future of our country sometimes receive only the rather haphazard attention of a handful of overworked men, while smaller, more detailed matters are being carefully worked on by a host of able people. One is uncomfortably reminded of the dinosaurs, which developed ganglia to control various parts of their massive bodies, but failed to develop much of a brain to guide their actions as a whole and, as a result, lost out in the Darwinian competition, despite their great size.

The need for a better-coordinated, more balanced, and more far-seeing approach to foreign policy has been widely recognized, but no solution to the problem has been found. Special bodies have been created from time to time to do long-range thinking and planning, but they tend to be either overlooked or caught up, like the rest of the government leaders, in day-to-day crises. Lower echelons, for safety's sake, are usually cautious and unimaginative. They stay carefully within established parameters of thought and expression. So-called policy papers tend to describe what has been policy rather than what it should be.

I do not know how this need for better policy formulation might best be met. Policy formulation requires a close awareness of the manifold day-to-day, nuts-and-bolts problems of foreign relations and at the same time sufficient detachment from them to be able to look at things in broad perspective and in thoughtful leisure. It also requires a close coordination with the President and the other top leaders in Washington who must assume responsibility for decisions on crises as they arise. The elements are to be found, but not together. An intimate awareness of the specific problems exists, but scattered broadly throughout the lower echelons of government. Among the general public are plenty of thoughtful people with the time to look at things in broad perspective. The problem is how to produce a proper blend of these two elements and bring this blend to the service of the President and the other decision makers.

To do this, I feel certain that it will take a much more determined and probably much larger effort than could be made by a small Policy Planning Staff in the State Department, or by a few staff workers for the harried members of the National Security Council at the White House, or by advisory panels and special task forces drawn from the general public. We should not expect that we can plan our foreign policies wisely and coordinate them effectively without devoting a reasonable amount of energy and resources to the effort.

Compared with what we as a nation put into getting a man to the moon, or amusing ourselves through television, or developing weapons to back up foreign policy, we put extremely little into deciding what foreign policy should be. Our government's budget for space exploration is close to $5 billion, but the budget for the whole State Department and its 119 embassies and 147 consulates is less than $400 million—not a tenth as much—and only a tiny part of this is devoted to the formulation of overall policy. The C.I.A. (Central Intelligence Agency), which has the primary function of collecting intelligence on which policy can be based and the secondary function of carrying out supplementary programs to support policy, employs thousands of able people and has a budget said to be in the billions, but not a hundredth as many people or as much money is devoted to the formulation of the policy itself.

2. *Some Guidelines for Foreign Policy*

Whatever the methods devised, however, for making policy and coordinating it, there are a few simple rules that should be observed. The most important is that American policy must be simple, straightforward, and clear. As I have said, we are by far the largest ship of state, and we must therefore hold to a simple, clear course. We are too large to try to be tricky or move about in devious ways. Such maneuvers may be possible for a dictator in a small country, though I doubt their utility even then. For us, they are most unwise. Too many other countries depend on us and our actions. It is important that they understand our intentions clearly. We must forego the small immediate advantage of trickiness for the larger long-range advantages of having others trust in us.

It is for this reason that I believe it is a mistake for our government to engage in clandestine operations (other than intelligence collection) anywhere in the world. The sort of covert political activity popularly associated with the C.I.A. is of value only in relatively weak and disrupted countries—and even then only for short-range purposes. Activities of this sort, however, do serious damage to confidence in the good faith and honesty of the United States elsewhere in the world, and I suspect that in the long run they have an adverse effect on our interests even in the countries where they seem to be temporarily effective. They confuse the people of such countries, often making them think the C.I.A. is the real government of the United States. They erode faith in our honesty and respect for the principles we claim to profess. Even in these countries, confidence in our honesty and good faith is probably our greatest asset. Thus on balance such covert activities are, I feel, clearly a net loss to us abroad, and, running counter as they do to our own concepts of morality, they probably do even more serious internal injury to us at home.

A second general principle of policy formulation is that it must be fully integrated and coordinated. Our defense relations, military commitments, and military presence abroad constitute extremely important aspects of our foreign relations that must be judged in the context of our total interests and actions and fitted in accordingly. There is a complicated problem of coordination with the Pentagon in Washington and with field commands abroad. Our foreign trade and other economic relations constitute another great area of American interest that must be fitted into the totality of our foreign relations and that calls for careful coordination with the Commerce Department and Treasury as well as with private American business. There are endless other aspects of American foreign relations, some extremely complicated or highly specialized, but all demanding careful coordination with the rest. What seems sensible within one restricted area may prove inconsistent with what seems sensible in another. We cannot afford to have actions in one field nullify those in another or undercut the general principles that we are trying to establish. Unless carefully orchestrated, American policies and actions abroad can all too easily produce confusing and irritating dissonance.

Achieving a harmonious orchestration of American foreign policy and our actions abroad is no easy problem. We need better techniques of coordination in Washington than the present mass of overlapping and constantly shifting interdepartmental coordinating committees and the overburdened members of the National Security Council, which is in a sense the top coordinating committee. In the field, there is need for even closer coordination. In the past there have been cases when in a single country the American military, the C.I.A., the A.I.D. mission, and the embassy all went their somewhat independent ways. Such absurdities have been for the most part corrected, but there is need for still closer integration. This is an additional reason why the C.I.A. should not be engaged in political activities but should be limited to its original function of intelligence gathering. There should be only one top representative of the United States government in any country, and this should, of course, be the ambassador. I say this with absolute conviction after a considerable term of experience as an ambassador. A.I.D. activities should be as much under the ambassador as any other activity of an embassy. The military also, in all their contacts with the foreign government and its people, should be completely under the control of the ambassador.

A third general principle is that we should free ourselves from the traditional concepts of diplomacy and adapt our foreign relations to the conditions of the late twentieth century. Most of the rules of diplomacy were standardized in the nineteenth century but reflect even more the conditions of the eighteenth century. As one who lived by them for more than five years, I can say that they are sometimes charming and even more often amusing. No simple professor could help but be gratified to find that he had suddenly been transformed into "Your Excellency." The ambassadorial pecking order, established by the date of presentation of one's credentials, must be witnessed to be believed. At a formal dinner party, not only are seating arrangements determined by it, but at the end each ambassador and his lady fall instinctively into this pattern in timing their departure.

All this is harmlessly quaint, I suppose, but we should not let it lull us into feeling that diplomacy is still what it was in the eighteenth or nineteenth century. It was originally the relations between sovereign heads of states and then grew into relations between their governments. In the present age of mass societies, it is even more the relations between peoples. It is, of course, still conducted between their respective governments, and at the core there remain formal diplomatic negotiations and treaties. But now most governments, if not always directly controlled by the people, are sensitive to their interests and attitudes in a way they were not a century or two ago. The international contacts they supervise are also vastly more complex than they were in the past. These contacts include enormously complicated fields—such as air routes and atomic energy—that were not even dreamed of a century ago.

All this means that modern diplomacy must be supported by many types of technical competence that the old diplomacy lacked, and it must also have whole new dimensions to cover the relations between peoples, rather than merely governments. American diplomacy has accommodated itself to these changes—but perhaps not yet fully enough. There is still a reluctance to develop adequate technical competence in the new fields, or if not that then a failure to integrate them fully into diplomacy as a whole. There is even greater reluctance to embrace wholeheartedly a people-to-people diplomacy. We are only beginning to accept the very important and central role of economic and technological aid in our relations with the less developed countries. We are still further from recognizing the importance of informational, cultural, and intellectual contacts in our relations not only with these countries but with all countries and particularly those that through democratic institutions do have governments that are controlled by the understanding and attitudes of the general public.

Attitudes of other peoples toward us, their understanding of us, and our understanding of them will probably do as much as military or economic relations to shape our future world environment. During my years in Japan, for example, I found that the traditional sort of diplomatic negotiations with the Japanese government offered very little problem, because the Japanese government was staffed by able and well-trained men with whom one could deal on a basic of clear understanding. Economic relations were more complex and difficult, raising as they did strong popular emotions in Japan, but they were reasonably manageable. The real problem, however, was popular understanding in Japan of American motivations and actions. Here lay the great bulk of the work for modern diplomacy in our relations with Japan.

In this sense, the work of the U.S.I.A. (United States Information Agency) was the most important activity of the embassy in Japan, but unfortunately this part of the embassy was perhaps least adequately prepared, lacking sufficient talent, funds, or even proper direction to do its job as well as it should have. For one thing, the whole U.S.I.A. function is not correctly conceived in Washington. Too often it is described as "telling the American story." It almost sounds as if we were trying to sell some new detergent. There are places in the world, no doubt, where a special effort must be made to spread accurate news about the United States. But this is not the situation in many parts of the world, including Japan, which is saturated with information from its own excellent mass media. Most people abroad are not interested in the "American story" as such. They are interested in themselves and in what America may mean to them and their future. What is needed is the development of mutual understanding between them and us and beyond that of useful knowledge, whether it is derived from the United States or elsewhere. This is the job not so much for newspapermen or salesmen as for thinkers, teachers, and persons with competence in various specialized fields of interest. It calls for people of the highest quality if the job is to be done well.

In developing knowledge and understanding between peoples, private citizens, of course, are probably more effective than governments. My own experience convinces me that in the informational, cultural, and intellectual fields, private citizens can do anything the government can, only better, and there are many useful activities they can perform that the government is barred from. The problem, however, is that private groups are not likely to have adequate financial resources to do what is needed. Perhaps government financing for private or semiprivate foundations would be part of the answer. There should be nothing clandestine about it, as was the case in C.I.A. activities of this sort. Even then, there would probably be a residue of such work —larger than what we are doing now—that would have to be undertaken directly by the government.

The financial inadequacies of the U.S.I.A. operation are serious. I found, for example, that many of the activities in Japan had pitifully insufficient budgets. A good case in point is afforded by the twelve very modest American Cultural Centers we have maintained in recent years in various parts of the country. They are highly appreciated by the local Japanese and often serve as the only official American representation in areas with populations larger than the average country in the U.N. Recently several of these centers were closed for lack of funds because of the Vietnam War. It should be noted that the total costs of the closed centers would not equal more than a fraction of the cost of maintaining a platoon of soldiers in Vietnam. I feel certain that these centers could do infinitely more in the long run for American interests than an additional platoon could in Vietnam.

Throughout the world we have shown a reluctance to put much effort or investment into information activities and cultural and intellectual exchanges. Budgets for this field, small though they are, undergo the most unfriendly scrutiny in Congress and suffer the most severe slashes. Not enough able people are attracted to the field, and those who are do not receive adequate training or support. In all ways, this is the end of the line in our foreign relations. But dollar for dollar and man for man, this is probably the most productive area of effort. Actually not many people or much money can be usefully devoted to it. This is all the more reason why the people in the field and their programs should both be of the highest quality. When we stop to think how much money and brainpower we as a nation devote to getting an American or two to land on the uninhabited moon, it seems tragically ludicrous that we devote so little to developing understanding between ourselves and the three billion other human beings who inhabit our own globe.

3. *The State Department*

I have suggested that the State Department has been undeservedly criticized for inadequacies in the formulation and coordination of foreign policy. Our foreign affairs are now too vast, too complicated, and too central to our national interests to be shoved in their entirety back under the roof of a single department of the government. Formulation of basic policies and over-all coordination can only be done at the presidential level and will require new mechanisms if they are to be done well. Still, the State Department, as the part of the government solely concerned with foreign relations, should play a special role in the formulation and coordination process in Washington, and its embassies should direct and coordinate a unified American policy abroad. To fulfill even these tasks, the State Department and its Foreign Service need to be decidedly strengthened.

Some would-be defenders of the Foreign Service, reacting to the flood of unfair criticism, have decried the fact that the old Foreign Service has been swamped by the addition of great numbers of peripheral experts and what they would feel are unnecessary, peripheral functions. I am afraid, however, that this attempted defense points in the wrong direction. These traditionalists are looking back with nostalgia to a simpler day, when a small, elite Foreign Service presided over a much more restricted and narrowly diplomatic relationship between the United States and foreign countries. That day and its concept of international relations are now gone.

The State Department and the Foreign Service must

handle much broader, much more complex, and much more diversified problems than in the days before the Second World War. To do this they must have more talent, more expert knowledge, more authority, and a broader concept of their role. I discovered in Tokyo how essential it was to have experts in many different fields, such as air routes, fisheries, and atomic energy, both in the State Department and in our embassy in Japan. Relations between Japan and the United States in such fields are so important and so complex that skilled specialists are called for. In a world that is rapidly coming closer together and is growing more complex even more rapidly, this proliferation of experts will undoubtedly continue.

Most people realize this fact and also the necessity for the State Department and Foreign Service to be deeply involved in our military relations abroad and in our foreign trade and other economic relations. There is, however, a tendency on the part of some traditionalists in the Foreign Service to draw back from the newer aspects of the new diplomacy. They wish to draw the line at getting involved in economic aid programs or in information work and cultural and intellectual activities. In many parts of the world, however, these are probably our most important relations. If they were to be subtracted from the State Department's functions, there would be very little of significance left for it to do.

The work of U.S.I.A. I found so vital in our whole diplomatic task in Japan that I considered our local U.S.I.A. staff to be as central and important a part of our embassy in Tokyo as the political or economic sections. At the time, this was considered a somewhat eccentric attitude. The more or less autonomous position of U.S.I.A. in Washington, as a sort of second-class member of the State Department family, seemed to me a mistake, causing many needless difficulties both in Washington and in the Tokyo embassy. While I had no experience with A.I.D. programs, I am inclined to feel that A.I.D.'s autonomous position is also a mistake. Both mistakes, I feel, are products of unjustifiable points of view: the traditionalists' disdain for these new activities and the desire of the State Department, as probably the least popular department of the government with Congress, to attempt to disassociate itself from its least popular activities.

If the State Department is to perform its role successfully it will require more adequate human and financial resources. It is the one department of the executive branch lacking any special interest groups or blocs of voters to give it domestic political support. Where the Commerce Department and Treasury have the support of business interests, the Labor Department that of organized labor, the Agriculture Department the support of farmers and food processors, and the Defense Department strong support from military contractors and the huge number of former servicemen and officers—many of them members of Congress—the State Department has no such fan clubs, and, presiding as it does over the least understood and most baffling aspects of national policy, it is the recipient primarily of brickbats from the public rather than bouquets. This public attitude, I fear, is reflected in Congress by niggardly and almost contemptuous treatment of the State Department. As compared with other major undertakings in our country, such as military defense, space exploration, television, or even the movie industry, we attempt to run our foreign relations on the proverbial shoestring.

Let me give a few minor but revealing examples from my personal experience. It would be hard to imagine a reputable American business corporation unable, because of lack of travel funds, to hold a conference of top executives on some important matter. A similar situation in the American military establishment would be unthinkable. But it is all too common that the top officers of the Department of State and its embassies must forego similar conferences or postpone important trips because of inadequate funds. To my amusement, I discovered that the Commander of the United States Forces, Japan, had for protocol purposes a large staff headed by a full colonel, but I, as the ambassador to Japan, with much larger and far more important protocol functions, had a staff that began and ended with a girl who had no training in this field. At the embassy in Tokyo, our numerous military attachés arrived for service after two years of special preparation in language and other matters, but many embassy officers, performing much more important functions, could not be given this training for lack of personnel and funds. Our U.S.I.A. staff, which probably needed language skills most of all, was even less well provided with them, and language training for the U.S.I.A. group was almost completely eliminated to save money and personnel for Vietnam. One wonders why the Air Force can contract for large research projects of interest to it through the Rand Corporation and other private agencies, but the State Department has no funds for comparable studies of its even more complex and nationally more important problems.

In such ways we reveal our lack of a sense of proportion. We are sensibly generous in our use of men and money for certain national undertakings but penurious in providing for the execution of our foreign policies and penny-pinching to the point of folly in providing for their formulation, direction, and coordination.

We must devote more of our abilities and energy to our foreign relations. They are of vital importance to our national well-being and possibly to our very existence. There is no reason why a nation as large and rich as ours cannot develop the expert knowledge and technical skills that are required to conduct these relations well. If we can afford to devote so much effort to exploring space or to amusing ourselves through television, we certainly can afford to supply the brainpower and energy needed for this much more important activity. We should ensure that all the talented people needed are attracted into foreign relations work, that they are given the best training possible, and that they are provided with all the support and funds required. If this were to be done, even on a lavish scale, we would still be devoting only an inconsequential percentage of our national resources to this work, and it would prove to be the wisest investment in our future that we could make.

The subject of training raises the old problem of the balance between experts and generalists in our foreign relations. The Foreign Service has prided itself on the general competence of its members. It has recognized the need for some specialized skills but has tended to fear that the specialist in a language and cultural area would develop "localitis," showing too parochial a point of view to be sound in broad policy matters.

The other side has pointed to the obvious need for specialized knowledge and language skills if our foreign affairs are to be competently handled. One might add that something more than mere factual knowledge is needed. Even more important is what might be called understanding, and this comes only after long and intimate contact with a people of a differing culture, and even then only by meeting them through their own language. If we as a nation are to act wisely and effectively in our relations with any country of radically different culture and language, we must give to adequate numbers of Americans the long training that is needed to become thoroughly at home in that culture and language. We cannot afford to continue to fly blind as we did when we entered on our heavy commitments to Korea and Vietnam with no real experts on either country. The quality and competence of our representation abroad is often as important as our policies. The way one does something can be even more important than what one does.

A seesaw battle has raged for years over the proper balance between geographic specialization and more general experience. Actually, the argument seems to me out of date.

The charge of localitis, I believe, is derived from an earlier period when Foreign Service Officers sometimes developed "fake" English accents and other foreign affectations that irritated their stay-at-home compatriots. So far as I can see, it applies very little today and least of all to Americans who have specialized in non-Western areas. If a man lacks a sense of proportion with regard to the country on which he specializes, this is likely to be the result of a basic personality failing that would show up whatever his field of interest. I do not personally know of a single case in which American interests were hurt by an American official's having developed too close an attachment to a non-Western country. But I have seen endless cases in which American interests were hurt seriously by ignorance about a country or insensitivity to the thinking and feeling of its people. At this stage in history, specialization is as necessary in our foreign relations as in everything else. We could not get along with just generalists in the natural sciences or in industry, and we cannot do this in the vastly important field of our relations with the outside world.

Of course, we do not face an either-or choice. Both specialists and generalists are needed, and most higher officers could well be a blend of the two. If the State Department and Foreign Service were adequately staffed, this would be possible. In most modern fields of endeavor, most persons start out as specialists of one sort or another and those who show the requisite abilities and temperament then move on to more generalized responsibilities. This might be a reasonable pattern for the Foreign Service too.

Actually, specialization of two different kinds is essential —in certain subjects, such as economics, aid, cultural relations, and the like, and in certain difficult languages and non-Western cultures. It is absurd for a country like ours not to have sufficient specialists of both types. There should be enough to permit specialists of each type to have had a chance to broaden themselves through other types of experience. It is poor economy for the country to stint on personnel and expert knowledge in this key matter of foreign relations. We should be at least as thorough in our training for this field as we are for defense.

4. *Education for Life in the Contemporary World*

More expert knowledge in government and better and more adequately staffed organs for formulating and executing policy, however, are not enough if we are to meet the challenge of our world position. This is a democracy, and the soundness of our foreign policy depends finally on the knowledge and understanding of the American people. However wise our experts may be, Congress will not fund their proposals unless its members feel that their constituents will support them. This is not just "democratic theory." I have seen it in operation time after time with regard to policy problems in which I was personally involved. The public must be reasonably well informed and understanding if our government is to be able to execute wise policies. In domestic matters, this situation may be attainable in most cases, because all our citizens are, at least by comparison, experts on the United States. In foreign affairs, particularly in policies dealing with a distant, complicated, and often mysterious-seeming area like Asia, it is a very large order. To fill it will take special efforts.

This problem does not merely concern the general public. In a way it is even more pressing with our top-level government officials. Members of the Cabinet and sub-Cabinet move in and out of Washington fairly rapidly. An Under Secretary or Assistant Secretary may be there only two years. During that period, he is a grossly overworked man, with little time to delve deeply into complex problems. The level of understanding he brings with him from his earlier education and general background will have to guide him in his decisions. This may be fine for domestic matters, but it is not likely to be adequate for judging our relations with Asia or other non-Western areas. Until men in these positions come into Washington with more understanding of the non-Western world than they now usually have, we are skating on very thin ice in policy decisions.

Again one is reminded of the Darwinian competition in which some species faded out because they proved unable to adapt to changing circumstances. The environment in which our nation lives has changed radically in recent decades. The isolation provided by great surrounding oceans has been eliminated by scientific advances. Instead of living in a relatively remote part of the Western world, we now find ourselves living in a greatly shrunken unitary world, in which non-Western peoples outnumber Occidentals by close to three to one.

The problem essentially is that our educational system remains geared to the political and cultural conditions of the nineteenth century. We educate our children only about ourselves and our own cultural heritage and then expect them to grow up and live successfully in a unitary world of many cultures. By dealing only with the Western tradition, we unconsciously indoctrinate our children with the idea that all other traditions are aberrant or not worth knowing. This may have been adequate for the nineteenth century when distances were great and the imperialist hold of the West on other regions made the Occident the only part of the world that really counted for us. Today, however, this approach to education is dangerously outdated, and it will get more unrealistic with each passing year.

We can compensate a little for our lack of basic education on Asia by efforts at the adult-education level. Various organizations like the Foreign Policy Association, numerous study groups, and careful reading can help, but such activities touch only a tiny fraction of the American people. In recent years, courses on Asia and other non-Western areas have proliferated in our better universities and colleges. Graduate schools turn out a steady stream of specialists on Asia, and fair numbers of undergraduates take at least one course on a non-Western civilization. The percentage increase in these activities during the past three decades has been astronomical, but they still affect only a small minority of each student generation. Efforts at the college and adult-education levels should, of course, be increased, but the fundamental need is to so modify elementary and secondary education that it prepares all our young people for life in the "one world" in which we now live.

A few outstanding secondary schools do have solid instruction on non-Western cultures, and some whole school systems are experimenting with additions to the curriculum for this purpose. A danger in the latter approach, however, is that the very fact that non-Western materials are "additional" to the regular curriculum may confirm the belief among children that any culture other than our own does everything in strange and backward ways and, therefore, is essentially "barbaric."

Our elementary and secondary education, backed up by a lot of home conditioning, tends to convey a very misleading impression of the history of mankind, confirming false assumptions that the West is and has been superior to the other civilizations of mankind, and that its nineteenth-century position of dominance over the rest of the world is natural and will continue indefinitely into the future. These are dangerous misconceptions for Americans to harbor in the second half of the twentieth century.

The typical schoolboy concept of history is likely to go along the following lines: Civilization got its obscure start in outlandish places like Egypt and Mesopotamia, which subsequently relapsed into barbarism, and only after it got into the hands of the Israelites and Greeks did it become true civilization. Greek civilization was passed on to Rome and the Judaic tradition to the Christianity its people adopted. Then this combined true civilization was passed to the North Europeans, and subsequently it moved to the North American continent, where it achieved its final flowering in us.

Other peoples figure in the story only as the barbarians who repeatedly attempted to stamp out civilization. The Egyptians and others oppressed the Israelites; the Persians tried to destroy Greece; barbarians (and here we distinguish between our own "noble" Germanic ancestors and the truly "barbaric" Asiatic Huns) did destroy Rome; the Saracens, the Mongol hordes, and the Turks all in turn threatened civilization but fortunately were repulsed. Happily the barbarians in time subsided into passive ignorance and poverty, in which state we, the bearers of the true torch of civilization, discovered them and ruled them, and now we find them a source of embarrassment and trouble, because they cause wars and revolutions and remain inconsiderately close to starvation. This picture may be overdrawn, but I believe it is essentially the impression many of our schools convey to their pupils.

We need to restructure our concept of the world and its history, so that children grow up learning about the whole experience of mankind that has produced the actual world in which we live. We need not slight our own Judeo–Greek–Roman–North-Europeans–American heritage. It is not only our own particular line of development but at this moment in history the most important one as well. But, by seeing that it has been paralleled and sometimes excelled by other lines of development, we will learn more about it as well as about other traditions and will become better prepared to live in our contemporary world of many cultures.

5. *Toward a World History*

There are, no doubt, many ways in which we can approach the problem of educating children for life in the twentieth-century world. Each of these would have to be adapted to the specific needs of the successive levels of schooling. For illustrative purposes, however, I have outlined below one way to approach a true world history. This is merely a postscript to this postscript chapter, leading away from our immediate policy problems in Asia, but perhaps serving to highlight the lack of perspective that has helped produce them.

For a true world history, I would suggest a presentation of the various technological and institutional levels that have spread one after the other throughout most of the world. Within that temporally stratified framework could then be woven the story of the major cultural traditions that have maintained their very distinct identities throughout all these different technological levels. We would start with the primitive hunting and gathering stage of human development, known as the Paleolithic. Next would come the early agricultural phase, with its pottery and more complex artifacts, which is known as the Neolithic and has survived into modern times in various remote corners of the world.

The Late Neolithic period saw the rise in widely separated parts of the world of little city-states and relatively large and highly centralized political units of considerable wealth and complexity. The chief centers of such developments were not just the valleys of the Nile and the Tigris and Euphrates but also the upper Indus Valley in the northwestern corner of the Indian subcontinent and the lower stretches of the Yellow River in North China. Similar stages of civilization were reached, though at a later time, by the Aztecs in Mexico and the Incas in Peru. In all cases, these civilizations prospered in treeless but reasonably well-watered areas, where agriculture could flourish but a heavy forest cover did not have to be combated. These cultures all showed marked technological and institutional similarities but also sharp cultural differences. Writing systems were developed in most, along with complex calendars, elaborate ceremonials, and the institution of divine kingship.

The use of bronze and then iron followed in the civilizations of Asia and Europe, but not of the Americas. The area of high culture also spread, and larger and richer social and political units were formed. There was now such complexity in these societies that speculation about the nature of society and about man's relationship to his environment was stimulated. The economies also were now rich and diversified enough to support people who could devote themselves to such speculation. In each of the areas of higher civilization, there was a rather sudden and glorious outburst of philosophic thought. The questions men grappled with were much the same in all these areas, but the answers often were quite different. This was the age of the Jewish prophets and Greek philosophers on the shores of the Mediterranean, of the early Indian philosophical works and of the Buddha in India, and of Confucius and the other Confucian, Taoist, and heterodox philosophers in China. The basic cultural traits that have persisted throughout history and still divide these civilizations so sharply had already become quite distinct.

Further technological development, including probably cheaper and better iron weapons that made mass armies of foot soldiers more effective than aristocratic warriors in chariots, led to the increasing size of political units and the appearance of great empires—the Persian, Macedonian, and Roman in the West, the Mauryan and its successor empires in India, and the Ch'in and Han in China. In all three areas this was a time of unprecedented power and wealth, but the period was characterized less by innovation in philosophy and culture than by the adaptation and development of earlier patterns. In the West, the Romans developed the impersonal institution of law; in East Asia, the Chinese, relying more on men of superior quality, developed the concept of a bureaucracy of merit.

These great empires all eventually fell, sometimes for similar reasons. Thereafter the story is a little harder to structure, no doubt because it becomes progressively more complex. There was a great spread of the area of higher civilization, primarily from treeless or lightly forested areas to those with more rainfall and therefore a heavier forest cover. This probably was the result of further technological and economic advances, particularly the growing availability of iron tools, especially the ax, which could subdue the forest growth. Western civilization spread to Northern Europe, into the areas that would in time be France, England, and Germany and more slowly into Scandinavia and Russia. In India, the higher civilization spread into the forested south and east and on into what are now the countries of Southeast Asia. In China it spread to the forested south and on beyond to North Vietnam and eastward to Korea and Japan.

Another major development of this period was the shift in the balance of power between foot soldiers and cavalry. The invention of the stirrup may have been vital to this, but it also may have reflected the spread of higher technology and institutions to people living in the peripheral areas of nomadic life and horse breeding. In any case, mounted nomads for the next several centuries figured large in history, pillaging settled communities, overthrowing empires, and founding even broader empires of their own, all the way from Korea to Eastern Europe and North Africa.

Another feature of this period was the splitting of Islam from the Judeo-Christian tradition of the West and the resultant division of the Western zone of civilization into two distinct halves.

A curious contrast within the various zones of higher civilization also developed at much the same time. Europe proved unable to recreate or maintain the classic pattern of empire, except on its Byzantine periphery, but in the other areas classic empires followed one after another, despite disruptions by the nomads. The rise of Islam gave stimulus to a vast expansion of empire as well as the faith, and for a while there was a glorious cultural revival within the Islamic area that far outshone Europe of that time. Indian empires rivaled the original Mauryan achievement and permitted the development of levels of wealth and power beyond anything Europe could then match. In China in particular, the restored pattern of empire was extremely successful. The bureaucratic system was perfected, the classical cultural heritage was carefully restudied and greatly enriched in a veritable renaissance, technology moved ahead, wealth accumulated, and China entered on its millennium of world leadership. Its magnificence inspired imitation on its periphery, and unified Korean, Japanese, and Vietnamese states developed as reflections of the Chinese empire pattern.

Another curious variation also developed in Western Europe and Japan—associated at least in the case of Europe with the inability to re-create genuine empires, and probably in both areas with their freedom from inundation by conquering nomadic horsemen. This was the system called feudalism, which in a sense reflected the dominance at this historical stage of the man on horseback, but in a more isolated and less centrally organized environment than that of the continuing empires. Feudalism also seems to have been a blend of the more advanced political concepts of the old empires (Roman law in the West and Chinese bureaucracy and law in Japan) with the more primitive tribal and personal concepts of organization of the Germanic peoples and the Japanese. In any case, these two areas went through a historical experience quite different from that of the rest of humanity and developed under feudalism certain traits that were quite distinct from those of the remaining old empires. From this experience seem to have emerged in Europe the early stages of the great technological and institutional changes that we call modernization. In Japan it seems to have produced the qualities that made modernization a much simpler matter there than in other Asian countries.

Because of the technological superiority the Europeans had achieved by early modern times, they were able to spread their sea power around the world and dominate the rich maritime trade, which hitherto had largely been between the heavily populated and rich lands of East, South, and West Asia. The Europeans were also able to appropriate for themselves most of the still lightly populated, primitive parts of the world—in particular North and South America and later Australia. In time, through their preponderant military and economic power, they established colonial or semicolonial control over most of the other zones of higher civilization. This then led to the nationalistic reaction of the non-Western countries in our own time and their determined efforts to catch up again with the West in technological skills, wealth, and power.

Meawhile the rapid technological and institutional changes of modernization continued at an accelerating pace in the West, presenting bewildering new problems to the modernized nations as well as to those just starting to modernize. And, of course, throughout all of history, the major cultural heritages and their many national subdivisions continued to grow and develop within their own traditions, while a tremendous acceleration in human mobility and communication greatly increased their influence on one another, thus speeding up and complicating the whole process of cultural change.

This is a very sketchy and all too haphazard outline of one possible approach to a more balanced history of mankind. There may be other and much better ways to give our children a more correct understanding of the world in which they live. In any case, however, we must stop instilling in them the idea that there is only one true line of civilization and all else is, if not barbaric, amusingly upside down. That sort of education may have been adequate in the nineteenth century, but a nineteenth-century education is not adequate preparation for life in the last third of the twentieth century —particularly in the United States with its worldwide responsibilities. We would not tolerate it in the field of the natural sciences. We should not tolerate it in the equally important field of the study of human civilization and the relations between nations.

This is no longer a purely Western or even Western-dominated world. China and India are by far the most populous countries on the globe. Japan is a major economic and cultural force, showing promise of soon becoming the third most powerful nation in the world. It, as well as Pakistan, Indonesia, and Brazil, overshadow in population the traditional great powers of Western Europe. The problems and wars that might blight our future are more likely to emerge from the unstable non-Western world than from the Occident.

New educational approaches at the elementary and secondary levels will take effect on our foreign policies only slowly, but our Asian problems—in fact, all our foreign policy problems—will be with us for a much longer time. An educational system designed for the twentieth century is probably our most basic need if we wish, over the long run, to get beyond Vietnam to a safer and mutually more beneficial relationship with Asia. We cannot go on ignoring so much of the world in which we live.

A Note About The Author

EDWIN O. REISCHAUER, since September 1966 a University Professor at Harvard University, served with distinction as United States Ambassador to Japan from 1961 to 1966. His mission was the culmination of long experience in East Asia. He was born in Tokyo in 1910 and lived in Japan until 1927, and he has returned many times since then for study and visits to Japan as well as to China, Korea, and other areas in the Far East. He received his A.B. degree from Oberlin College in 1931 and his Ph.D. from Harvard in 1939. In the interval he studied at the universities of Paris, Tokyo, and Kyoto and in Korea and China. He became an instructor at Harvard in 1939, an associate professor in 1945, and professor of Japanese history in 1950. During World War II he served with the rank of lieutenant colonel in the Military Intelligence Service of the War Department General Staff, and he was awarded the Legion of Merit. He has also worked for the Department of State in the Division of Far Eastern Affairs. He was director of the Harvard-Yenching Institute from 1956 to 1961 and president of the Association for Asian Studies from 1955 to 1956. Among his books are: *Japan Past and Present* (1947; new and revised editions 1952, 1964); *The United States and Japan* (1950, 1957, 1965); *Wanted: An Asian Policy* (1955); with J. K. Fairbank, *East Asia: The Great Tradition* (1960); and with J. K. Fairbank and A. M. Craig, *East Asia: The Modern Transformation* (1965)

A Note On The Type

The text of this book was set on the Linotype in a face called TIMES ROMAN, designed by Stanley Morison for *The Times* (London), and first introduced by that newspaper in 1932.

Among typographers and designers of the twentieth century, Stanley Morison has been a strong formative influence, as typographical adviser to the English Monotype Corporation, as a director of two distinguished English publishing houses, and as a writer of sensibility, erudition, and keen practical sense.

The book was composed, printed, and bound by The Haddon Craftsmen, Inc., Scranton, Pennsylvania.